REPORT

ON THE

TAX LEVIES

OF THE

CITY OF NEW YORK

FOR THE YEARS 1899 TO 1914, INCLUSIVE

PRESENTED TO THE

BOARD OF ESTIMATE AND APPORTIONMENT

BY

WILLIAM A. PRENDERGAST
COMPTROLLER

DEPARTMENT OF FINANCE

BUREAU OF MUNICIPAL INVESTIGATION AND STATISTICS

JANUARY, 1916

REPORT

ON THE

TAX LEVIES

OF THE

CITY OF NEW YORK

FOR THE YEARS 1899 TO 1914, INCLUSIVE

PRESENTED TO THE

BOARD OF ESTIMATE AND APPORTIONMENT

BY

WILLIAM A. PRENDERGAST

COMPTROLLER

DEPARTMENT OF FINANCE

BUREAU OF MUNICIPAL INVESTIGATION AND STATISTICS

JANUARY, 1916

90966-16-500

DEPARTMENT OF FINANCE

THE CITY OF NEW YORK

BUREAU OF MUNICIPAL INVESTIGATION AND STATISTICS.

December 28, 1915.

To the Board of Estimate and Apportionment, The City of New York:

Gentlemen—In order to ascertain accurately the total amount of deficiencies in taxes levied upon real and personal property, arising since January 1, 1898, the date of consolidation, an exhaustive examination was begun early in 1914, involving an analysis of the tax accounts for all levies from 1899 to and including 1913, as shown on the books in the several borough offices under the immediate jurisdiction of the Receiver of Taxes and the Collector of Assessments and Arrears.

On October 29, 1914, in partial compliance with your resolution of February 4th, 1910, there was submitted to your board a report covering all deficiencies in the product of taxes which had arisen since consolidation, together with all reservations and provisions for funding the same. To show the extent and nature of these deficiencies, there was included in this report an analytical statement showing in connection with each levy under review: (a) the amount of the levy, (b) the net collections, (c) the deficiencies, according to character, and (d) the uncollected balance at December 31, 1913, this information being subdivided as between real estate taxes and personal taxes.

Owing to the lack of time and because of a faulty system of account keeping in vogue prior to 1907, it was not possible to obtain an analysis of these tax levies in which the taxes included under the heading of real estate were segregated into the three component classes of (1) real estate (lands and buildings), (2) real estate of corporations and (3) special franchises.

Soon after the submission of this report, in order to comply more fully with your resolution of February 4th, 1910, as large a force of accountants as could be effectively utilized was assigned to the work of segregating the real estate taxes. The examination was extended to include the tax levy for the year 1914, and the analysis of the prior levies was brought down to December 31 of that year.

The results of this inquiry are presented in the summary tables, marked "A" to "G," and in the accompanying statements, marked "I" to "XVI."

An outline of the general plan and design of the main tables, together with an explanation of the several elements included therein, is set forth in the succeeding paragraph.

TABLES OF TAX LEVIES FROM 1899 TO 1914.

In order that the final results of this inquiry might adequately and completely disclose every important aspect relative to the imposition and subsequent liquidation of each tax levy from 1899 to 1914, it was found necessary to analyze the transactions relating thereto into the following elements:

(1) As to the imposition:

  (a) the amount of the tax levy, by year of imposition.

(2) As to disposition and liquidation:

  (a) the amount of taxes collected, less refunds and over and double payments.

  (b) The amount of taxes rendered uncollectible and therefore not realized, by reason of:

    (1) Discounts or rebates allowed to taxpayers in consideration of the prompt payment of taxes.

    (2) Remissions and cancellations of invalid taxes, and

    (3) Deductions from special franchise taxes allowed under the provisions of section 48 of the tax law.

  (c) The amount remaining uncollected at December 31, 1914, if any.

In addition these elements have been collated and classified with respect to the following constituent and collateral subdivisions:

(1) According to general character of property against which tax was levied.

(2) According to borough in which tax was raised.

(3) According to the year in which transaction was made.

An outline of the structure of these tables and the nature of the facts relating to each levy that the respective parts are designed to exhibit are shown in the following plan concerning the classification of the several elements, viz:

Part 1—Classification according to general character of property against which tax was levied, viz:

(a) Real Estate (Lands and Buildings);

(b) Real Estate of Corporations;

(c) Special Franchises;

(d) Personal Property.

Part 2—Classification according to boroughs.

Part 3—Classification according to general character of taxable property and according to borough, being a consolidation of the facts shown separately in Parts 1 and 2.

In addition to these three parts, there are appended to the main table for each levy, two supplementary tables supporting, amplifying and recapitulating the facts shown in Part 1, as follows:

Part 1a—Showing all transactions from date of imposition to December 31, 1914, classified according to general character of taxable property, and further analyzed according to year in which transactions were made.

Part 1b—Recapitulation, combining the several classes of tax shown in the preceding table (1a), and summarizing the transactions of the entire levy according to year of occurrence.

For statistical purposes and to facilitate comparison, tables expressing the ratios of the several elements to one another have been subjoined to the summary tables, as follows:

(1) Showing the percentage of each class of tax to the whole levy;

(2) Showing the percentage of each levy raised in each borough;

(3) Showing the percentage of taxes collected, for each class of tax and for each borough;

(4) Showing the percentage of taxes lost by reason of discounts allowed, cancellations of invalid taxes, and deductions from special franchise taxes under section 48 of the tax law;

(5) Showing the percentage of each class of tax remaining uncollected at December 31, 1914.

Each table, therefore, consists of three main parts and two supplementary parts, each part exhibiting a particular phase or combination of two or more phases, and the table as a whole presenting a complete picture of the progress of each tax levy in all its important aspects, in analytical and summary form, from the time of its imposition to December 31, 1914.

The summary statements A and B contain the same information as those numbered from I to XVI, but with the levies of the sixteen years assembled in order to exhibit the transactions of all the years in one total as affecting the different classes of taxes, as well as the operation in each of the several boroughs.

The summary tables C, D, E, and F are designed upon the same general principles as those previously described, but instead of exhibiting the entire action of each levy the transactions affecting all levies are set forth according to the year in which they took place. Each of these four summary tables has reference to one of the several classes of the general tax. Table G. shows in recapitulated form the total of the four classes of taxes levied and the combined transactions affecting all levies segregated according to year of occurrence.

FACTS CONCERNING THE LEVY AND COLLECTION OF TAXES.

Although the act of the legislature consolidating the various communities now comprising The City of New York became operative January 1, 1898, no general tax levy covering the five boroughs constituting the greater City was imposed until the latter part of the year 1899, for the expenses of that year. The year 1899 has since become a natural and convenient dividing line for transactions affecting tax levies, for the reason that facts relating to each tax levy imposed since 1899 are comparable, having been imposed upon the same area of land and under practically similar conditions. The former municipalities comprised within the present boroughs of Brooklyn, Queens and Richmond levied taxes in advance. Therefore the taxes for the year 1898 were levied in 1898 only in the Boroughs of Manhattan and The Bronx, which together constituted the former City of New York.

Summary Statement of Total Taxes Levied from 1899 to 1914, and Net Collections Thereon to December 31, 1914.

(A) Classified According to General Character of Taxable Property.

	Amount Levied.	Per Cent. of Specific Class of Tax to Total Amount of Taxes Levied.	Net Collections.	Per Cent. of Net Collections of Each Class to Total Net Collections.	Per Cent. of Net Collections of Each Class to Taxes Levied.
Real Estate (Lands and Buildings)	$1,500,317,270 42	85.24	$1,454,449,207 05	90.12	96.94
Real Estate of Corporations	24,614,113 56	1.40	20,209,258 08	1.25	82.10
Special Franchise ...	94,546,583 16	5.37	56,193,312 34	3.48	59.43
Total Real Estate	$1,619,477,967 14	92.01	$1,530,851,777 47	94.85	94.53
Personal Property ..	140,678,030 87	7.99	83,089,436 67	5.15	59.07
	$1,760,155,998 01	100.00	$1,613,941,214 14	100.00	91.70

(B) Classified According to Boroughs.

	Amount Levied.	Per Cent. of Borough Levies to Total Levies.	Net Collections.	Per Cent. of Net Collections from Each Borough to Total Net Collections.	Per Cent. of Net Collections from Each Borough to Taxes Levied.
Manhattan	$1,207,000,058 78	68.57	$1,116,411,150 53	69.17	92.50
The Bronx	107,203,445 67	6.09	97,543,617 70	6.04	90.99
Brooklyn	352,302,201 59	20.02	317,607,979 81	19.68	90.15
Queens	75,260,787 30	4.28	66,307,435 59	4.11	88.12
Richmond	18,389,504 67	1.04	16,071,030 51	1.00	87.39
	$1,760,155,998 01	100.00	$1,613,941,214 14	100.00	91.70

The total amount of taxes levied on real and personal property for the years 1899 to 1914 aggregates $1,760,155,998.01. Of this sum, $1,619,477,967.14 was levied on real estate, which includes land and buildings, real estate of corporations and special franchises, and $140,678,030.87 was levied on personal property. Thus, of the general property taxes *levied* during the period under review, 92.01 per cent. were laid upon real estate and 7.99 per cent. on personal property. When viewed from the standpoint of actual collections resulting from these levies, the ratios obtained are somewhat different. The total net collections to December 31, 1914, on account of all taxes levied upon real and personal property from 1899 to 1914 aggregated $1,613,941,214.14. Of this amount, $1,530,851,777.47, or 94.85 per cent., were collections on account of real estate taxes, and $83,089,436.67, or 5.15 per cent., were collections on account of personal taxes. Comparing specific collections with specific levies, we find that in connection with real estate taxes 94.53 per cent. of the taxes levied were collected to December 31, 1914, while, during the same period, only 59.07 per cent. of the personal taxes were collected.

During the same period the budget, as adopted, increased from $95,209,959.84 in 1899 to $192,995,551 in 1914, an increase of 102.70 per cent. The fact that the tax levy did not increase as rapidly as did the budget is accounted for by the relatively great increase in the receipts of the general fund. It might be here explained that in determining the amount to be raised by taxation on the general property within the city limits, the law provides that the estimated revenues of the general fund shall be deducted from the amount of the budget, giving as the amount of the tax levy the difference between the amount of the budget and the estimated receipts of the general fund.

In the tax levies prior to 1907 it was customary to add to the sum determined to be raised by taxation an amount equal to 2 per cent. of such tax levies to cover deficiencies in the product, although during those years the charter allowed three per cent. of the aggregate amount of the tax to be included to provide for deficiencies. For 1907 and subsequent years deficiencies in the product of tax levies were provided for by inclusion in the budget. In order, therefore, to make the 1899 budget comparable with the budget of 1914 it is necessary to add to the 1899 budget, as adopted, the amount included in the tax levy of that year to cover deficiencies in the product of tax levies.

The revenues of the general fund increased from $9,026,191.26 in 1899 to $43,235,-935.35 in 1914, an increase of over 379.06 per cent. This increase is most largely accounted for by the enactment of a law in 1903, which permitted the surplus revenues of the Sinking Fund for the Redemption of the City Debt (No. 1) to be invested in general fund bonds, the proceeds of which were paid into the general fund for the reduction of taxation. Since the assets other than those invested in general fund bonds will be sufficient to meet all liabilities of the said sinking fund, the general fund bonds held by it will be cancelled at maturity.

Comparing the amount of the tax levy at the beginning of the period under review, viz., 1899, with the amount of the tax levy at the end of the period, viz., 1914, we find that it has increased from $86,180,076.53 in 1899, to $150,503,514.53 in 1914, an increase of 74.64 per cent.

Following is a statement of comparison showing the several elements of the tax levy of 1899 and of 1914, together with the related percentage of increase or decrease:

Statement of Comparison, Tax Levy of 1899 *and Tax Levy of* 1914. *Showing the Elements of Each Tax Levy Classified (A) According to General Character of Taxable Property, and (B) According to Borough, Together with the Percentages of Increase and Decrease.*

	Levy of 1899.	Levy of 1914.	Percentage of Increase or *Decrease.
(A) According to Class of Tax—			
Real Estate (Lands and Buildings)...	$70,422,015 41	$133,831,562 06	90.04
Real Estate of Corporations..........	2,383,822 75	3,339,684 26	40.09
Special Franchises	†..........	7,248,956 94	†45.86
Total Real Estate................	$72,805,838 16	$144,420,203 26	98.36
Personal Property	13,374,238 37	6,083,311 27	*54.51
	$86,180,076 53	$150.503,514 53	74.64
(B) According to Boroughs—			
Manhattan	$62,814,741 81	$96,778,936 70	54.07
The Bronx	3,236,607 56	11,759,491 12	232.12
Brooklyn	15,459,721 79	31.472,676 10	103.57
Queens	3,600,792 88	8,902,777 94	146.96
Richmond	1,068,212 49	1,589,632 67	48.81
	$86,180,076 53	$150.503,514 53	74.64

†Comparison of special franchises made with levy of 1900, which was the first year in which special franchises were taxed. The amount of this levy for the year 1900 was $4,969,748 58.

From the foregoing tabulation, it will be seen that the tax levy on real estate increased from $72,805,838.16 in 1899 to $144,420,203.26 in 1914, an increase of 98.36 per cent. In the same period the tax levy on personal property decreased from $13,374,238.37 in 1899 to $6,083,311.27 in 1914, *a decrease of* 54.51 *per cent.* Much of the decrease in the yearly levy of personal taxes has been due to legislation eliminating from the classes of property formerly taxable under the general property tax law the following: mortgages, shares of national and state banks and trust companies, and evidences of secured debts. Of the three classes of property defined by law as real estate, the tax levy on lands and buildings shows the greatest increase, viz., 90.04 per cent.

When viewed from the standpoint of borough divisions, the tax levy for the Borough of The Bronx shows the greatest increase, viz., 232.12 per cent., while the tax levy for the Borough of Richmond shows the smallest increase, viz., 48.81 per cent.

DISCOUNTS.

Discounts are rebates or deductions from the gross tax allowed to the taxpayer in consideration of the prepayment of taxes. These discounts are losses in the product of the tax levy and create deficiencies which were provided for in the same manner as uncollectible taxes, pursuant to chapters 208 and 209 of the Laws of 1906.

The total loss in the levies through discounts allowed to taxpayers in consideration of the prompt payment of taxes during the period from 1899 to 1914, inclusive, aggregates $4,985,002.37. This sum represents approximately 39-100 of one per cent. of the total taxes levied for the years during which these discounts were allowed. Of this amount, $4,096,451.63 was allowed during the nine years from 1899 to 1907, and represents over 51-100 of one per cent. of the total taxes levied during these years. From 1908 to 1911, inclusive, no discounts were allowed, the charter having been amended early in 1908, abolishing the allowance of discounts. The practice of allowing discounts for the prepayment of taxes was resumed in 1912, when the present plan of providing for the payment of the tax levy in two equal installments was put into operation as a means of effecting a saving in interest costs to the city. For the three years ended 1914 the discounts allowed to the taxpayers for the prepayment of taxes aggregate $888,550.74, or 19-100 of one per cent. of the total taxes levied during these three years.

Prior to 1912 taxes for the current year became due and payable on the first Monday in October. Prior to 1908, personal and real estate taxes paid during October were entitled to a discount or rebate for prompt payment, which was calculated at the rate of six per cent. per annum from the date of payment in October to the first day of the succeeding December. During the month of November payments were subject neither to discount nor penalty. To taxes paid during the month of December a penalty of one per cent. was added, while taxes paid after the 31st day of December were subject to an interest charge calculated at the rate of seven per cent. per annum from the first Monday in October to the date of payment.

The enactment of chapter 447 of the Laws of 1908 amended sections 914 to 917 of the Greater New York Charter and abolished the allowance of discounts. From 1908 to 1911 taxes were due and payable, as before, on the first Monday in October, and all payments made before the first day of November were subject to neither discount nor penalty. Payments of taxes made after the first day of November were subject to an interest charge calculated at the rate of seven per cent. per annum from the first Monday in October to the date of payment.

It will be noted that although taxes became due and payable on the first Monday in October, expenditures for the current year began immediately after the first day of that year. Hence, in order to finance itself, the city was compelled to borrow on short-term revenue bonds to meet current expenses. These bonds were issued in anticipation of the collection of taxes. The city therefore starts the fiscal year on January 1 with practically no money, and aside from the miscellaneous receipts of the General Fund, receives no money until the collection of the current tax levy is begun. Inasmuch as no funds were available to meet the expenses of the current year until the revenue from taxes was received, the borrowings of the city in theory approximated the expenses for the first nine months of the year. This kind of financing called for a considerable interest expense on account of the large sums of money the city was thus compelled to borrow.

The enactment of chapter 455 of the Laws of 1911 amended the charter with respect to the levy and collection of taxes, substituting for the annual levy of taxes due and payable on the first Monday in October of the year for which the taxes are raised, a provision which permitted the levy and collection of taxes in semi-annual installments. Under the provisions of this law the date upon which taxes became due and payable was advanced from the first Monday in October to the first day of May, with respect to taxes upon all personal property and one-half of all taxes upon real estate, the second or final half of the real estate tax being due and payable on the first day of November. In order to encourage the prepayment of the second half of the tax upon real estate this law revived the practice of allowing discounts for the prepayment of taxes. It permits the deduction of a discount at the rate of four per cent. per annum from the date of payment to November 1 on all payments on real estate of the second or final half of the tax when such payment is made between the first day of May and the first day of November. All personal property taxes are due and payable May 1 and no discounts are allowed. All taxes or portions remaining unpaid after the first days of June and December, respectively, are subject to a charge for interest at the rate of seven per cent. per annum, calculated from the date on which the respective parts became due and payable to the date of payment.

As a result the city now begins to receive its revenue from the tax levy approximately five months earlier than it did under the scheme in vogue prior to 1912. The borrowings of the city through the sale of short-term revenue bonds, issued in anticipation of the collection of taxes, have been greatly reduced, and as a consequence a great reduction in the interest cost has been effected.

CANCELLATIONS.

Cancellations may be made by order of the court, by Comptroller's order and through remission by the Board of Taxes and Assessments. The Commissioners of the Sinking Fund are authorized by section 221A of the Charter to cancel taxes levied against certain classes of real estate, but when such action is taken it is supplemented by a Comptroller's order, so that when entered it takes that form. Section 248 of the Charter was amended by the 1915 Legislature so as to permit the Board of Estimate and Apportionment to authorize the cancellation of uncollectible personal taxes. There have been no cancellations under this new law up to the present time, but it is expected that the Board of Estimate and Apportionment will be requested to authorize the elimination of a considerable amount of personal taxes in the near future.

Section 897 of the charter invests the Board of Taxes and Assessments with power to remit or reduce any tax assessed upon real or personal property. This board may remit or reduce a tax upon real property if it is found erroneous or excessive, but may remit or reduce a tax on personal property only under certain prescribed conditions, clerical errors or inability of the person aggrieved to appear while the record of assessed valuation is open for correction, through illness or absence from the city. Remissions of taxes which have been made by the Board of Taxes and Assessments are included under the heading "Cancellations" in the analysis of general tax levies appended hereto.

Property of the United States and of the State of New York; and property of the City of New York held for a public use; the real property of religious or eleemosynary corporations or associations, and some other classes of property are exempted from taxation for general purposes by section 2 of the tax law. A tax is frequently levied, through error, improper description or otherwise, against exempt property, and it being clearly invalid, the Comptroller may direct its cancellation.

Section 906 of the charter contains a provision as to when a certiorari to review or correct any final determination of the Board of Taxes and Assessments shall be allowed by the Supreme Court or any justice thereof. Under this provision property owners who are not satisfied with the valuation of their property as determined by the Board of Taxes and Assessments appeal to the court for correction. If the court decides that the assessment is incorrect an order is issued directing its reduction and the amount of the corresponding tax is a cancellation.

The public service corporations have secured material reductions of their special franchise taxes by court order. During the earlier years of the special franchise taxes, ordinary real estate was assessed at less than its full value and the courts decided that special franchises should be assessed at the same proportion of their value that prevailed in the case of other real estate. This decision has compelled the cancellation of several million dollars of special franchise taxes.

ORDINARY REAL ESTATE.

The greatest portion of taxes levied since consolidation has been assessed upon the "ordinary real estate," which is also designated as Real Estate (Lands and Buildings), in order to distinguish it from the "Real Estate of Corporations" and "Special Franchises." This class of property has been assessed with 85.24 per cent. of all the general taxes levied from 1899 to 1914. The aggregate net collections from all classes of taxes beginning with the levy of 1899 to and including December 31, 1914, was $1,613,941,214.14, of which the ordinary real estate paid 90.12 per cent., or $1,454,449,207.05.

From the following statement of real estate taxes levied from 1899 to 1914, classified according to boroughs, it will be seen that 67.75 per cent. of the total taxes levied fall upon the Borough of Manhattan, and that 68.39 per cent. of the total net collections are paid by that borough. In each of the other boroughs the percentage of the amount collected is less than the borough's proportion of the total amount levied. Comparing the borough collections with the borough levies, the proportion collected in Manhattan is greater than that of any other borough, 97.87 per cent. of the total amount of taxes levied upon real estate (lands and buildings) having been collected in Manhattan, and the next highest percentage indicated being in Brooklyn, where 96.27 per cent. was collected. In this respect the poorest showing is in the Borough of Queens, where only 90.81 per cent. of the taxes levied upon real estate (lands and buildings) was collected.

Summary Statement of Real Estate (Land and Buildings) Taxes—Levies, 1899 *to* 1914, *Classified According to Boroughs, Showing Net Collections Thereof to December* 31, 1914.

	Amount Levied, 1899 to 1914.	Per Cent. of Borough Levies to Total Levies.	Net Collections to December 31, 1914.	Per Cent. of Borough Collections to Total. Collections,	Per Cent. of Borough Collections to Borough Levies.
Manhattan	$1,016,409,477 02	67.75	$994,763,816 90	68.39	97.87
The Bronx	93,343,443 04	6.22	88,108,315 27	6.06	94.40
Brooklyn	307,937,245 44	20.52	296,429,315 80	20.38	96.27
Queens	66,759,199 08	4.45	60,621,545 79	4.17	90.81
Richmond	15,867,905 84	1.06	14,526,213 29	1.00	91.54
	$1,500,317,270 42	100.00	$1,454,449,207 05	100.00	96.94

Not only does the ordinary real estate (lands and buildings) produce the largest portion of revenues raised by taxation in the City of New York, but the relative amount collected as compared with that levied is greater. The collections for the sixteen years ended December 31, 1914, for this class of taxes aggregated $1,454,449,-

207.05 out of $1,500,317,270.42, the grand total of all the levies. The collections, therefore, comprise 96.94 per cent. of the levies, and as the discounts and cancellations were only 64/100 of one per cent., the balance uncollected at December 31, 1914, is only 2.42 per cent. of the amount of the levies.

The following summary statement exhibits the real estate (lands and buildings) taxes levied from 1899 to 1914 in each year, with all the transactions affecting them and the uncollected balances as at December 31, 1914:

Summary Statement of Real Estate Taxes (Lands and Buildings), Levies 1899 *to* 1914, *Showing All Transactions from Date of Imposition to December* 31, 1914.

Year of Levy.	Amount of Levy.	Net Collections to Dec. 31, 1914.	Per Cent. of Net Collections to Levy.	Total Discounts and Cancellations.	Per Cent. of Discounts and Cancellations to Levy.	Uncollected Balance at Dec. 31, 1914.	Per Cent. of Uncollected Balance to Levy.
1899..	$70,422,015 41	$69,541,933 40	98.75	$689,600 34	.97	$190,481 67	.28
1900..	66,109,359 06	65,334,549 66	98.83	652,662 29	.99	122,147 11	.18
1901..	69,985,905 58	69,186,222 04	98.86	635,953 77	.91	163,729 77	.23
1902..	70,550,043 48	69,885,907 36	99.06	534,592 56	.76	129,543 56	.18
1903..	64,149,021 06	63,337,896 94	98.73	650,739 68	1.02	160,384 44	.25
1904..	72,220,078 07	71,126,351 80	98.49	859,366 36	1.19	234,359 91	.32
1905..	73,585,830 65	72,419,350 81	98.42	870,062 99	1.18	296,416 85	.40
1906..	79,496,876 72	78,285,383 70	98.48	921,041 82	1.15	290,451 20	.37
1907..	85,580,422 29	84,283,593 28	98.48	929,532 96	1.09	367,296 05	.43
1908..	99,989,581 80	98,996,321 20	99.01	468,653 98	.47	524,606 62	.52
1909..	105,933,728 87	104,884,587 50	99.01	355,533 35	.33	693,608 02	.66
1910..	115,080,167 28	113,644,252 81	98.75	297,306 02	.26	1,138,608 45	.99
1911..	124,845,014 59	122,440,590 94	98.08	303,022 16	.24	2,101,401 49	1.68
1912..	133,946,733 95	129,943,520 55	97.02	567,789 71	.42	3,435,423 69	2.56
1913..	134,590,929 55	127,781,818 29	94.94	475,319 17	.35	6,333,792 09	4.71
1914..	133,831,562 06	113,356,926 77	84.70	375,304 90	.28	20,099,330 39	15.02
	$1,500,317,270 42	$1,454,449,207 05	*96.94	$9,586,482 06	*.64	$36,281,581 31	*2.42

*Average.

Except in the last four years shown there is less than one per cent. remaining uncollected of any year's levy. Out of the $36,281,581.31 uncollected for the sixteen years over $33,000,000 applies to the last five years. More than 99 per cent. of the levies for 1902, 1908 and 1909 have been collected, and over 98 per cent. in all the years, except 1912, 1913 and 1914. In course of time and through tax sales it seems safe to assume that the collections will reduce the percentages of uncollected taxes for the latter years to approximately the same percentages shown for the earlier years.

REAL ESTATE OF CORPORATIONS.

The title "Real Estate of Corporations" includes private rights of way of public service corporations and the improvements thereon. Subdivision 3 of section 2 of the tax law defines the terms "land," "real estate" and "real property" to be:

"The land itself above and under water, all buildings and other articles and structures, substructures and superstructures, erected upon, under or above, or affixed to the same; all wharves and piers, including the value of the right to collect wharfage, cranage or dockage thereon; all bridges, all telegraph lines, wires, poles and appurtenances; all supports and inclosures for electrical conductors and other appurtenances upon, above and under ground; all surface, underground or elevated railroads, including the value of all franchises, rights or permission to construct, maintain or operate the same in, under, above, on or through, streets, highways or public places * * *."

This section of the tax law directs that a franchise, right, authority or permission in, upon, under or above any street, highway, public place or public waters, as well as the tangible property thereon shall be known for the purpose of taxation as a "special franchise." This leaves the private rights of way of franchise-holding corporations, together with the tangible property thereon for assessment as "real estate of corporations."

In 1899 and prior years the taxes on tangible property, which are now levied under the designation "special franchise," were imposed as "real estate of corporations." For 1900, the first year of the levy of a special franchise tax, the amount levied upon real estate of corporations was $679,268.62, as compared with a levy of $2,383,822.75 for the previous year. This reduction was more than offset, however, by the taxes levied upon special franchises, which were $4,969,748.58.

The total amount of taxes levied upon the real estate of corporations for the sixteen years from 1899 to 1914 was $24,614,113.56, of which $20,209,258.54 was collected, or 82.10 per cent. of the total levy. The following table shows the transactions in respect to "real estate of corporations taxes" for the levies from 1899 to 1914, to the 31st of December, 1914:

Summary Statement of Real Estate of Corporations Taxes, Levies 1899 *to* 1914, *Showing All Transactions from Date of Imposition to December* 31, 1914.

Year of Levy.	Amount of Levy.	Net Collections to Dec. 31, 1914.	Per Cent. of Net Collections to Levy.	Total Discounts and Cancellations.	Per Cent. of Discounts and Cancellations to Levy.	Uncollected Balance at Dec. 31, 1914.	Per Cent. of Uncollected Balance to Levy.
1899..	$2,383,822 75	$1,949,891 84	81.80	$422,935 01	17.74	$10,995 90	.46
1900..	679,268 62	456,599 30	67.23	213,370 61	31.41	9,298 71	1.36
1901..	721,067 36	473,746 74	65.70	242,257 03	33.60	5,063 59	.70
1902..	704,173 61	454,168 57	64.50	245,127 74	34.81	4,877 30	.69
1903..	418,359 13	386,387 98	92.37	23,771 90	5.68	8,199 25	1.95
1904..	495,012 08	458,574 32	92.64	21,640 06	4.37	14,797 70	2.99
1905..	493,042 26	450,089 70	91.29	26,168 13	5.31	16,784 43	3.40
1906..	759,212 75	502,720 01	66.21	240,254 08	31.65	16,238 66	2.14
1907..	1,048,897 83	683,740 45	65.19	348,093 19	33.19	17,064 19	1.62
1908..	1,445,418 58	829,098 58	57 37	601,616 90	41.62	14,703 10	1.01
1909..	1,289,192 17	1,034,750 98	80.27	233,231 69	18.09	21,209 50	1.64
1910..	1,555,696 39	1,165,777 67	74.94	311,103 07	19.99	78,815 65	5.07
1911..	2,881,065 74	2,592,410 74	89.98	193,855 82	6.73	94,799 18	3.29
1912..	3,109,931 58	2,769,887 67	89.07	217,124 89	6.98	122,919 02	3.95
1913..	3,290,268 45	2,957,817 50	89.89	43,623 66	1.33	288,827 29	8.78
1914..	3,339,684 26	3,043,596 03	91 14	12,441 03	.37	283,647 20	8.49
	$24,614,113 56	$20,209,258 08	*82.10	$3,396,614 81	*13.80	$1,008,240 67	*4.10

*Average.

There was uncollected at December 31, 1914, only 4.10 per cent. of the total amount of real estate of corporations taxes levied for the sixteen years under consideration. The amount remaining uncollected is $1,008,240.67, of which $790,-192.69 applies to the years 1911, 1912, 1913 and 1914, which will be considerably reduced by future collections, together, possibly, with some cancellations.

The following summary statement of the Real Estate of Corporations taxes shows the net collections on all levies from 1899 to December 31, 1914, classified according to boroughs. It will be noted from this statement that the Borough of The Bronx produces 25.83 per cent. of the total taxes levied on the real estate of corporations. Only 6.44 per cent. of the personal taxes, 4.77 per cent. of the special franchise taxes, and 6.22 per cent. of the taxes on ordinary real estate (lands and buildings) are assessed upon property in that borough.

Summary Statement of Real Estate of Corporations Taxes, Levies 1899 *to* 1914, *Classified According to Boroughs, Showing Net Collections Thereof to December* 31, 1914.

Borough.	Amount Levied. 1899 to 1914.	Per Cent. of Borough Levies to Total Levies.	Net Collections to December 31, 1914.	Per Cent. of Borough Collections to Total. Collections,	Per Cent. of Borough Collections to Borough Levies.
Manhattan	$10,194,996 74	41.42	$7,547,480 90	37.35	74.03
The Bronx........	6,357,259 85	25.83	5,880,194 66	29.10	92.50
Brooklyn	4,157,497 35	16.90	3,258,968 88	16.13	78.39
Queens	3,269,746 13	13.28	2,921,741 00	14.45	89.35
Richmond	634,613 49	2.57	600,873 10	2.97	94.69
	$24,614,113 56	100.00	$20,209,258 54	100.00	82.10

SPECIAL FRANCHISES.

Subdivision 3 of section 2 of the General Tax Law defines a special franchise as the right, authority or permission to construct, maintain or operate in, under, above, on or through a public highway a structure intended for public use, and the franchise is deemed to include the value of the tangible property so situated.

Special franchises were made taxable property for the first time in the history of the state by the enactment of chapter 712 of the Laws of 1899. Prior to the passage of the law corporations and others operating a public utility through a public highway were taxed only on the value of the tangible property used in connection with the operation of such public utility. By the enactment of the special franchise tax law the state board of tax commissioners was empowered "to annually fix and determine the valuation of each special franchise subject to assessment in each city, town or village" of the state and transmit it to the local taxing authorities for inclusion in the tax rolls of the district. In fixing the value of the special franchise the state board of tax commissioners was directed by law to include the value of both tangible and intangible property. Section 48 of the law further defined special franchises as "real property" and directed that all sums in the nature of a tax paid by the owner of the special franchise to a municipality be deducted from the amount of the tax due and payable under the provisions of this act.

The first assessment under the new law was made in 1900, and the report of the state board of tax commissioners showed an increase of $135,000,000 over and above the taxable property theretofore assessed by the local department of taxes and assessments. The increase was due mainly to the value of the intangible franchise, which prior to the enactment of the franchise tax law was exempt from local taxation.

In order to test the validity of the tax and the constitutionality of the law several of the public service corporations operating in the city obtained separate writs of certiorari to review the respective assessments. This was the beginning of a long and persistent opposition waged by the corporations through the several courts of the state, and carried for final determination to the Supreme Court of the United States.

The granting of the writs of certiorari to review the assessments resulted in an order in each proceeding appointing a referee to take and report to the Supreme Court of the State such evidence upon the several issues raised by the companies contesting the validity of the tax and attacking the constitutionality of the law as might be adduced before him, with his findings of fact and conclusions of law thereon.

The referee, Judge Earl, after taking many pages of evidence, made separate and complete findings of fact appropriate to each proceeding and reached the legal conclusion in each case "that chapter 712 of the Laws of 1899 is a valid and constitutional enactment, practicable and operative, and that it gave authority to the defendants (State Board of Tax Commissioners) to assess the relators' (companies') special franchise for the purpose of taxation; that the relator had a hearing and due process of law before the defendants upon the review of the assessment * * * and was not deprived of any of its legal or constitutional rights; that it was lawful to assess as one franchise the franchise right, authority or permission which the relator had in the streets of New York and which it operated as one system; that to equalize its assessment with the assessment of other real property in the City of New York the relator is entitled to a deduction," the amount being named in each proceeding, "and that the assessment as thus reduced must be taken as the value of the relators' special franchise for the purposes of assessment and taxation under the act."

The Supreme Court of the State adopted the finding both of fact and law, as made by the referee. The companies at once appealed to the Appellate Division of the third and fourth departments, which affirmed as to the facts, but reversed as to the law, the decision of the Supreme Court, upon the ground that the statute in question was in violation of the "home rule" provision of the constitution. The State Board of Tax Commissioners thereupon appealed to the Court of Appeals.

On April 28, 1903, the Court of Appeals unanimously decided that the order of the Appellate Division should be reversed and the judgment of the Supreme Court affirmed. The Court of Appeals, in addition to overruling the contention that the act is impracticable and incapable of execution, etc., decided that the act does not violate the principle of home rule embodied in the State Constitution, because it creates a *new* system of taxation, requiring officers with new functions to enforce it, and that tangible property connected with the special franchises is an inseparable part thereof, forming an entity which was never before taxable by local assessors.

Declaring that the courts had erred in declining to hold that the act of 1899 was in contravention of the provisions of the Federal Constitution, the companies carried the case to the Supreme Court of the United States, where, on May 29, 1905, the power of the state to tax special franchises was definitely settled and the decision of the Supreme Court of New York affirmed.

Summary Statement of Special Franchise Taxes, Levies 1900 *to* 1914, *Classified According to Boroughs, Showing Net Collections Thereof to December* 31, 1914.

Borough.	Amount Levied, 1900 to 1914.	Per Cent. of Borough Levies to Total Levies.	Net Collections to December 31, 1914.	Per Cent. of Borough Collections to Total Net Collections.	Per Cent. of Borough Collections to Borough Levies.
Manhattan	$67,084,678 56	70.95	$41,733,052 54	74.27	62.22
The Bronx	4,511,603 38	4.77	2,737,676 77	4.88	60.68
Brooklyn	19,522,538 81	20.65	9,514,642 18	16.92	48.74
Queens	2,842,164 30	3.01	1,898,929 66	3.38	66.81
Richmond	585,598 11	.62	309,011 19	.55	52.77
Total.......	$94,546,583 16	100.00	$56,193,312 34	100.00	59.43

The following statement exhibits in summary form the transactions of all the levies of special franchise taxes from 1900, the first year of the levy of such taxes, to December 31, 1914. The total of discounts and cancellations, $27,285,210.13, includes $10,851,264.80 deducted pursuant to the provisions of section 48 of the law, because the corporations assessed had paid that amount for some other purpose, and under the law were held by the courts to have credit for it toward their special franchise taxes. These deductions are shown under a special heading in the main tables appended hereto.

Summary Statement of Special Franchise Taxes, Levies 1900 *to* 1914, *Showing all Transactions from Date of Imposition to December* 31, 1914.

Year of Levy.	Amount of Levy.	Net Collections to Dec. 31, 1914.	Per Cent. of Net Collections to Levy.	Total Discounts, Cancellations and Deductions.	Per Cent. of Discounts, Cancellations and Deductions to Levy.	Uncollected Balance at Dec. 31, 1914.	Per Cent. of Uncollected Balance to Levy.
1900....	$4,969,748 58	$2,676,255 01	53.85	$2,028,307 62	40.82	$265,185 95	5.33
1901....	4,925,291 84	2,535,381 50	51.48	2,308,004 91	46.86	81,905 43	1.66
1902....	5,049,106 47	2,587,204 00	51.24	2,403,071 20	47.60	58,831 27	1.16
1903....	3,360,543 42	2,256,769 12	67.16	1,065,572 88	31.71	38,201 42	1.13
1904....	3,837,072 69	2,636,034 33	68.69	1,160,436 93	30.25	40,601 43	1.06
1905....	4,546,986 43	2,994,727 19	65.87	1,516,839 60	33.36	35,419 64	.77
1906....	5,394,041 11	3,469,898 19	64.33	1,877,394 53	34.81	46,748 39	.86
1907....	7,005,982 97	3,975,051 26	56.74	2,669,775 77	38.11	361,155 94	5.15
1908....	8,017,257 50	4,620,239 16	57.63	2,898,216 24	36.15	498,802 10	6.22
1909....	8,022,692 92	4,836,514 92	60.29	3,060,546 18	38.15	125,631 82	1.56
1910....	8,249,097 11	4,531,843 22	54.94	1,926,009 95	23.35	1,791,243 94	21.71
1911....	8,325,934 55	4,963,035 09	59.61	1,643,686 63	19.74	1,719,212 83	20.65
1912....	7,602,095 47	5,155,994 16	67.82	758,344 88	9.97	1,687,756 43	22.21
1913....	7,991,775 16	4,815,443 34	60.26	982,522 98	12.29	2,193,808 84	27.45
1914....	7,248,956 94	4,138,921 85	57.10	986,479 83	13.61	2,123,555 26	29.29
	$94,546,583 16	$56,193,312 34	*59.43	$27,285,210 13	*28.86	$11,068,060 69	*11.71

*Average.

The following table classifies under appropriate headings each of the total discounts, cancellations and deductions under section 48 of the tax law, as shown in the preceding table:

Summary Statement of the Discounts, Cancellations and Deductions Under Section 48 of the Tax Law, Affecting Special Franchise Taxes, from Date of Imposition to December 31, 1914.

Year of Levy.	Discounts.	Cancellations.	Deductions Under Section 48, Tax Law.	Total Discounts, Cancellations and Deductions.
1900	$134 25	$1,753,691 32	$274,482 05	$2,028,307 62
1901	61 34	1,757,035 13	550,908 44	2,308,004 91
1902	130 23	1,837,558 76	565,382 21	2,403,071 20
1903	1,091 56	524,541 02	539,940 30	1,065,572 88
1904	1,765 40	597,987 45	560,684 08	1,160,436 93
1905	3,837 73	913,969 32	599,032 55	1,516,839 60
1906	873 88	1,228,506 97	648,013 68	1,877,394 53
1907	6,527 13	1,906,478 24	756,770 40	2,669,775 77
1908	....	2,017,443 90	880,772 34	2,898,216 24
1909	....	2,077,676 06	982,870 12	3,060,546 18
1910	....	997,017 52	928,992 43	1,926,009 95
1911	....	664,326 18	979,360 45	1,643,686 63
1912	19,239 31	91,744 18	647,361 39	758,344 88
1913	14,594 07	....	967,928 91	982,522 98
1914	17,714 38	....	968,765 45	986,479 83
Totals	$65,969 28	$16,367,976 05	$10,851,264 80	$27,285,210 13

Out of the total levies upon special franchises of $94,546,583.16, the net collections amounted to $56,193,312.34, or 59.43 per cent., and on December 31, 1914, there remained uncollected $11,068,060.69. Of this balance uncollected, $9,515,577.30 is applicable to the last five years and constitutes 85.97 per cent. of the total.

PERSONAL TAXES.

An important feature connected with an analysis of the tax levies, and one which merits the careful attention of those interested therein, is the experience of The City of New York in connection with the imposition and subsequent collection of taxes on personal property. The securing of reliable detailed data concerning the results of the taxation of personal property has not always been easy of accomplishment. To students of taxation and to others interested in the operation of the personal property tax and its productiveness, the statements and tables submitted herewith are likely to arouse special interest, in view of the fact that herein are exhibited, in analytical and in summary form, much valuable data concerning the city's experience with the personal property tax, covering a period of sixteen years, viz., 1899 to 1914, inclusive.

As pointed out in a preceding paragraph, the total taxes levied on personal property during the sixteen-year period under review aggregated $140,678,030.87, which sum represents over 7.99 per cent. of all the general property taxes levied during this period. In the following statement there is presented a comparison of the relative proportion of real property taxes levied with the relative proportion of personal property taxes levied in each of the five boroughs during the years from 1899 to 1914. Reference to this statement shows that, with the exception of the Borough of Manhattan, the total personal taxes levied in each borough are a relatively smaller proportion of the total personal tax levies than the corresponding proportion of real estate taxes levied in such borough during this period. Thus, the Borough of The Bronx, in which 6.44 per cent. of the total real estate tax was levied, contributed only 2.12 per cent. of the personal property tax levied. A similar observation may be made with respect to the Boroughs of Brooklyn, Queens and Richmond. Referring to the situation in the Borough of Manhattan, it may be pointed out that the total real estate levies for the period 1899 to 1914 aggregated $1,039,689,152.32, or 67.53 per cent. of the total real estate levies for the entire city, while the total personal tax levies aggregated $113,310,906.46, or 80.55 per cent. of the total personal taxes levied in the entire city during the same period.

Comparative Statement Showing Total Real Estate (All Classes) and Total Personal Property Taxes, Levies 1899 *to* 1914, *Classified according to Boroughs.*

Borough.	Total Real Estate Taxes Levied 1899 to 1914.	Per cent of Borough Levies to Total Amount Levied.	Total Personal Property Taxes Levied 1899 to 1914.	Per cent of Borough Levies to Total Amount Levied.	Total Taxes Levied 1899 to 1914.	Per cent of Borough Levies to Total Amount Levied.
Manhattan	$1,093,689,152 32	67.53	$113,310,906 46	80.55	$1,207,000,058 78	68.57
The Bronx	104,212,306 27	6.44	2,991,139 40	2.12	107,203,445 67	6.09
Brooklyn	331,617,281 60	20.48	20,684,919 99	14.70	352,302,201 59	20.02
Queens	72,871,109 51	4.50	2,389,677 79	1.70	75,260,787 30	4.28
Richmond	17,088,117 44	1.05	1,301,387 23	.93	18,389,504 67	1.04
Total	$1,619,477,967 14	100.00	$140,678,030 87	100.00	$1,760,155,998 01	100.00

Perhaps the most discussed feature of the personal property tax has been its relative productiveness. Out of the total personal taxes levied during the 16-year period from 1899 to and including 1914, to-wit, $140,678,030.87, the sum of $83,089,-436.67, or 59.07 per cent., was collected to December 31, 1914.

Analyzing these collections according to the boroughs in which they were made, it will be observed that the best results, when viewed from the standpoint of relative productiveness, were obtained in the Borough of Manhattan, where, with a total borough levy equal to 80.55 per cent. of the total personal taxes levied for the period under review, the collections equalled 63.87 per cent. of such borough levies. In comparing the collections in the Borough of Manhattan with those in the other boroughs of the City, we find that the Borough of Manhattan has produced more than 87.10 per cent. of the total revenue derived from the imposition of the personal property tax during the past 16 years. A summary of these facts is presented in the following table:

Summary Statement of Personal Taxes, Levies 1899 *to* 1914, *Classified According to Boroughs, Showing Net Collections Thereof to December* 31, 1914.

Borough.	Amount Levied, 1899 to 1914.	Per Cent. of Borough Levies to Total Levies.	Net Collections to December 31, 1914.	Per Cent. of Borough Collections to Total Net Collections,	Per Cent. of Borough Collections to Borough Levies.
Manhattan	$113,310,906 46	80.55	$72,366,800 65	87.10	63.87
The Bronx	2,991,139 40	2.12	817,431 00	.98	27.33
Brooklyn	20,684,919 99	14.70	8,405,052 95	10.12	40.63
Queens	2,389,677 79	1.70	865,219 14	1.04	36.21
Richmond	1,301,387 23	.93	634,932 93	.76	48.79
Total	$140,678,030 87	100.00	$83,089,436 67	100.00	59.07

The following table exhibits in summary form the city's experience in connection with the imposition and subsequent disposition of personal property taxes from 1899 to 1914.

As pointed out in a preceding paragraph, it will be noted that 59.07 per cent. of the total personal taxes levied from 1899 to 1914 was collected to December 31, 1914. Of the remaining sum, aggregating nearly 41 per cent. of the total personal taxes levied during this 16-year period, $356,388.80 was lost through discounts or rebates allowed to taxpayers in consideration of the prompt payment of taxes, and personal taxes aggregating $9,566,786.69 were remitted and cancelled because they were invalid and their collection could not be legally enforced. These two amounts represent 7.05 per cent. of the total personal taxes levied during this period. But this figure by no means represents the total loss or deficiency in the product of the personal tax levies imposed during this period, and it will be observed by reference to the statement submitted hereunder that there remained uncollected on the books of the City of New York at December 31, 1914, the large sum of $47,665,218.71, or approximately 33.88 per cent. of all the personal property taxes levied from 1899 to 1914. This sum, with the exception of a relatively small part of the uncollected balance outstanding of the levy of 1914, may be considered as uncollectible and placed in the same category as the $9,923,375.49 herein previously referred to as representing the amount of taxes lost through discounts allowed and the cancellation of invalid taxes.

From the foregoing survey, it may be confidently stated that at least 40 per cent. of the total personal property taxes levied from 1899 to 1914 inclusive will prove uncollectible. These uncollectible balances, with other deficiencies in the product of real estate tax levies, have from time to time been provided for either by the issuance of corporate stock, as authorized by chapter 208 of the Laws of 1906, or since 1907 by inclusion in the annual budget, as provided by section 248 of the Greater New York Charter, as amended by chapter 209 of the Laws of 1906.

Summary Statement of Personal Taxes, Levies 1899 *to* 1914, *Showing All Transactions from Date of Imposition to December* 31, 1914.

Year of Levy.	Amount of Levy.	Net Collections to Dec. 31, 1914.	Per Cent. of Net Collections to Levy.	Total Discounts and Cancellations.	Per Cent. of Discounts and Cancellations to Levy.	Uncollected Balance at Dec. 31, 1914.	Per Cent. of Uncollected Balance to Levy.
1899..	$13,374,238 37	$8,482,110 45	63.43	$506,180 91	3.78	$4,385,947 01	32.79
1900..	10,780,825 69	7,596,842 00	70.47	537,997 18	4.99	2,645,986 51	24.54
1901..	12,609,537 08	7,027,001 63	55.74	1,177,376 40	9.33	4,405,159 05	34.93
1902..	11,925,231 36	6,332,010 10	53.09	1,355,322 95	11.37	4,237,898 31	35.54
1903..	9,703,850 94	4,954,753 97	51.06	891,877 03	9.19	3,857,219 94	39.75
1904..	9,516,240 66	4,969,875 44	52.23	241,114 31	2.53	4,305,250 91	45.24
1905..	10,354,826 68	4,691,347 71	45.31	1,163,035 81	11.23	4,500,443 16	43.46
1906..	8,444,962 83	4,379,701 89	51.87	734,200 73	8.69	3,331,060 21	39.44
1907..	8,312,366 93	4,503,438 48	54.18	739,629 38	8.89	3,069,299 07	36.93
1908..	7,088,825 73	4,364,782 69	61.58	559,066 49	7.88	2,164,976 55	30.54
1909..	7,497,019 70	4,555,089 19	60.76	552,205 17	7.37	2,389,725 34	31.87
1910..	6,589,809 14	4,620,985 70	70.12	510,284 43	7.75	1,458,539 01	22.13
1911..	6,185,744 49	4,389,227 78	70.96	508,715 25	8.22	1,287,801 46	20.82
1912..	6,297,944 75	4,436,406 77	70.44	341,411 69	5.42	1,520,126 29	24.14

Year of Levy.	Amount of Levy.	Net Collections to Dec. 31, 1914.	Per Cent. of Net Collections to Levy.	Total Discounts and Cancellations.	Per Cent. of Discounts and Cancellations to Levy.	Uncollected Balance at Dec. 31, 1914.	Per Cent. of Uncollected Balance to Levy.
1913..	5,913,295 25	3,958,393 84	66.94	51,689 70	.87	1,903,211 71	32.19
1914..	6,083,311 27	3,827,469 03	62.91	53,268 06	.88	2,202,574 18	36.21
Total.	$140,678,030 87	$83,089,436 67	*59.07	$9,923,375 49	*7.05	$47,665,218 71	*33.88

*Average.

The following statement shows the amount of personal taxes collected in each year from 1899 to 1914, both inclusive, subdivided as follows: (a) The amount collected each year on account of the levy made during the year of the levy, (b) the amount collected each year on account of the levy made during the year preceding, (c) the amount collected each year on account of the levy made two years prior to the date of collection, (d) the amount collected each year on account of the levies made 3 years or more prior to the year of collection:

Statement of Personal Tax Collections from 1899 *to December* 31, 1914, *Showing Proportion of Each Year's Collections Which Was Made on Account of* (*a*) *Current Levy,* (*b*) *Preceding Levy,* (*c*) *Next Preceding Levy and* (*d*) *All Prior Levies.*

Year of Collection.	Current Levy.	Preceding Levy.	Next Preceding Levy.	All Prior Levies.	Total Collections.	Per cent. of Current Levy Collected.	Per cent. of Preceding Levy Collected.	Per cent. of Next Preceding Levy Collected.
1899	$7,342,551 04	....	....	....	$7,342,551 04	54.90	...	...
1900	6,689,831 18	$769,489 64	....	....	7,459,320 82	62.05	5.75	...
1901	5,929,471 57	673,315 96	$155,924 76	....	6,758,712 29	47.03	6.25	1.17
1902	5,601,909 95	886,307 54	146,784 02	$143,393 95	6,778,395 46	46.98	7.03	1.36
1903	4,346,476 44	580,642 26	120,237 82	62,100 59	5,109,457 11	44.79	4.87	95
1904	4,442,472 45	481,438 25	88,918 50	81,253 24	5,094,082 44	46.68	4.97	.74
1905	4,217,726 40	432,782 09	86,280 16	116,850 83	4,853,639 48	40.73	4.55	.88
1906	3,856,659 12	370,920 85	66,279 68	36,525 29	4,330,384 94	45.67	3.59	.69
1907	3,933,844 29	433,939 80	62,449 96	18,136 71	4,448,370 76	47.33	5.14	.60
1908	3,867,200 66	471,902 18	50,476 57	38,140 26	4,427,719 67	54.55	5.68	.60
1909	4,055,233 14	443,716 29	66,842 51	62,166 31	4,627,958 25	54.09	6.26	.80
1910	4,352,344 03	450,252 41	40,915 84	37,014 61	4,880,526 89	66.05	6.00	.58
1911	4,124,719 80	231,018 91	38,200 50	18,901 59	4,412,840 80	66.68	3.50	.51
1912	4,237,469 75	221,157 83	30,881 31	16,609 27	4,506,118 16	67.29	3.58	.47
1913	3,787,029 43	158,890 56	34,304 51	16,191 93	3,996,416 43	64.05	2.52	.55
1914	3,827,469 03	171,364 41	40,046 46	24,062 23	4,062,942 13	62.92	2.89	.64
	$74,612,408 28	$6,777,138 98	$1,028,542 60	$671,346 81	$83,089,436 67	*53.03	*5.04	*.79

*Average.

Until the enactment of chapter 601 of the Laws of 1915 no express authority existed in law for eliminating from the books of The City of New York or cancelling from the tax rolls these uncollectible items, and the city was therefore compelled to carry the same on its books, although in many instances the deficiencies in the city's accounts due to these losses have been fully funded either through the issue of corporate stock or by budget appropriation. In order to rid the city's books of those items which had proved to be uncollectible after every legal means for their collection had been exhausted, the enactment of chapter 601 of the laws of 1915 was secured. This amendment to the charter gave to the Board of Estimate and Apportionment the authority, upon the advice of the Corporation Counsel and with the concurrence of the Comptroller, to cancel on the records of the city the personal taxes that have been deemed by it to be uncollectible. Under the provisions of this law the city will be enabled to eliminate from its tax rolls every uncollectible item that has been so adjudged, so that the balances carried as uncollected at any given date will represent collectible items of personal taxes or those which are in process of collection.

This inquiry, involving the analysis, reconciliation and reconstruction of several hundred tax accounts, many of which contain transactions extending over a period of more than fifteen years, is the first comprehensive undertaking of this kind that has been made in the Department of Finance. As a result there has been produced for the first time a complete and detailed record of the city's experience in connection with the imposition and collection of all tax levies from 1899 to and including 1914.

This investigation will, it is hoped, prove a valuable guide in the future administration of the finances of the city, as indicating:

1. The productivity of each class of tax levied and the probable proportion of receipts from both current and prior levies within particular periods after imposition of the tax; also the relative productivity of the several boroughs.

2. The extent of probable deficiencies or losses through discounts and remissions and the cancellation of invalid or uncollectible taxes, especially marked in personal tax levies.

Respectfully,

WM. A. PRENDERGAST, Comptroller.

TABLE

Summary of Tax Levies, 1899 *to* 1914, *Inclusive, Classified According*

	Amount of Levy.	Collections. Total.	Collections. Less Refunds and Over and Double Payments.	Collections. Net.	Discounts.
			Part I.—Classified According to General		
Real Estate (Lands and Buildings) ..	$1,500,317,270 42	$1,456,670,355 35	$2,221,148 30	$1,454,449,207 05	$4,498,820 06
Real Estate of Corporations	24,614,113 56	20,373,169 87	163,911 79	20,209,258 08	63,624 23
Special Franchise..	94,546,583 16	57,689,975 57	1,496,663 23	56,193,312 34	65,969 28
Personal Property.	140,678,030 87	83,476,989 89	387,553 22	83,089,436 67	356,588 80
Grand Totals..	$1,760,155,998 01	$1,618,210,490 68	$4,269,276 54	$1,613,941,214 14	$4,985,002 37
				Part II.—Classified	
Manhattan	$1,207,000,058 78	$1,119,466,896 11	$3,055,745 58	$1,116,411,150 53	$3,748,353 73
The Bronx	107,203,445 67	97,724,948 67	181,330 97	97,543,617 70	222,718 75
Brooklyn	352,302,201 59	318,419,638 86	811,659 05	317,607,979 81	828,901 11
Queens	75,260,787 30	66,494,951 47	187,515 88	66,307,435 59	142,005 83
Richmond	18,389,504 67	16,104,055 57	33,025 06	16,071,030 51	43,022 95
Total	$1,760,155,998 01	$1,618,210,490 68	$4,269,276 54	$1,613,941,214 14	$4,985,002 37
			Part III.—Classified According to Boroughs		
Manhattan.					
Real Estate (Lands and Buildings) ..	$1,016,409,477 02	$996,301,971 08	$1,538,154 18	$994,763,816 90	$3,356,648 84
Real Estate of Corporations	10,194,996 74	7,598,051 30	50,570 86	7,547,480 44	18,913 17
Special Franchise..	67,084,678 56	42,984,011 25	1,250,958 71	41,733,052 54	53,125 53
Personal Property..	113,310,906 46	72,582,862 48	216,061 83	72,366,800 65	319,666 19
Total	$1,207,000,058 78	$1,119,466,896 11	$3,055,745 58	$1,116,411,150 53	$3,748,353 73
The Bronx.					
Real Estate (Lands and Buildings) ..	$93,343,443 04	$88,242,527 16	$134,211 89	$88,108,315 27	$195,573 65
Real Estate of Corporations	6,357,259 85	5,888,436 35	8,241 69	5,880,194 66	20,388 60
Special Franchise ..	4,511,603 38	2,776,101 06	38,424 29	2,737,676 77	4,807 71
Personal Property..	2,991,139 40	817,884 10	453 10	817,431 00	1,948 79
Total	$107,203,445 67	$97,724,948 67	$181,330 97	$97,543,617 70	$222,718 75
Brooklyn.					
Real Estate (Lands and Buildings)...	$307,937,245 44	$296,840,337 67	$411,021 87	$296,429,315 80	$783,364 13
Real Estate of Corporations	4,157,497 35	3,319,041 62	60,072 74	3,258,968 88	10,241 08
Special Franchise...	19,522,538 81	9,692,434 93	177,792 75	9,514,642 18	5,564 46
Personal Property..	20,684,919 99	8,567,824 64	162,771 69	8,405,052 95	29,731 44
Total	$352,302,201 59	$318,419,638 86	$811,659 05	$317,607,979 81	$828,901 11
Queens.					
Real Estate (Lands and Buildings)...	$66,759,199 08	$60,737,076 31	$115,530 52	$60,621,545 79	$126,972 20
Real Estate of Corporations	3,269,746 13	2,966,767 50	45,026 50	2,921,741 00	10,061 23
Special Franchise..	2,842,164 30	1,918,258 97	19,329 31	1,898,929 66	2,144 20
Personal Property..	2,389,677 79	872,848 69	7,629 55	865,219 14	2,828 20
Total	$75,260,787 30	$66,494,951 47	$187,515 88	$66,307,435 59	$142,005 83
Richmond.					
Real Estate (Lands and Buildings)...	$15,867,905 84	$14,548,443 13	$22,229 84	$14,526,213 29	$36,261 24
Real Estate of Corporations	634,613 49	600,873 10	....	600,873 10	4,020 15
Special Franchise...	585,598 11	319,169 36	10,158 17	309,011 19	327 38
Personal Property..	1,301,387 23	635,569 98	637 05	634,932 93	2,414 18
Total	$18,389,504 67	$16,104,055 57	$33,025 06	$16,071,030 51	$43,022 95

* Of this amount approximately $45,000,000 is uncollectible. For more specific statement

A.

to Boroughs and General Character of Taxable Property.

Cancellations.	Deductions Under Section 48, Tax Law.	Total.	Balance Uncollected at Dec. 31, 1914.	Percentages. Borough and Specific Levy to Total Levy.	Net Collections to Levy.	Total Discounts, Cancellations and Deductions to Levy.	Uncollected Balance to Levy.
Character of Taxable Property.							
$5,087,662 00	....	$9,586,482 06	$36,281,581 31	85.24	96.94	.64	2.42
3,332,990 58	....	3,396,614 81	1,008,240 67	1.40	82.10	13.80	4.10
16,367,976 05	$10,851,264 80	27,285,210 13	11,068,060 69	5.37	59.43	28.86	11.71
9,566,786 69	....	9,923,375 49	*47,665,218 71	7.99	59.07	7.05	33.88
$34,355,415 32	$10,851,264 80	$50,191,682 49	$96,023,101 38	100.00	91.70	2.85	5.45
According to Boroughs.							
$25,530,251 38	$6,480,952 33	$35,759,557 44	$54,829,350 81	68.57	92.50	2.96	4.54
1,572,760 17	515,788 37	2,311,267 29	7,348,560 68	6.09	90.99	2.16	6.85
6,192,761 94	3,781,113 48	10,802,776 53	23,891,445 25	20.02	90.15	3.07	6.78
823,309 64	73,410 62	1,038,726 09	7,914,625 62	4.28	88.12	1.38	10.50
236,332 19	....	279,355 14	2,039,119 02	1.04	87.39	1.53	11.08
$34,355,415 32	$10,851,264 80	$50,191,682 49	$96,023,101 38	100.00	91.70	2.85	5.45
and General Character of Taxable Property.							
$3,561,806 11	....	$6,918,454 95	$14,727,205 17	57.75	97.87	.68	1.45
2,223,309 57	....	2,242,222 74	405,293 56	.58	74.03	21.99	3.98
13,049,716 68	$6,480,952 33	19,583,794 54	5,767,831 48	3.81	62.22	29.19	8.59
6,695,419 02	....	7,015,085 21	33,929,020 60	6.43	63.87	6.18	29.95
$25,530,251 38	$6,480,952 33	$35,759,557 44	$54,829,350 81	68.57	92.50	2.96	4.54
$209,165 44	....	$404,739 09	$4,830,388 68	5.30	94.40	.43	5.17
345,614 18	....	366,002 78	111,062 41	.36	92.50	5.75	1.75
664,058 15	$515,788 37	$1,184,654 23	589,272 38	.26	60.68	26.26	13.06
353,922 40	....	355,871 19	1,817,837 21	.17	27.33	11.89	60.78
$1,572,760 17	$515,788 37	$2,311,267 29	$7,348,560 68	6.09	90.99	2.16	6.85
$986,629 27	....	$1,769,993 40	$9,737,936 24	17.50	96.27	.57	3.16
565,264 66	....	575,505 74	323,022 73	.23	78.39	13.84	7.77
2,404,540 78	$3,781,113 48	6,191,218 72	3,816,677 91	1.11	48.74	31.71	19.55
2,236,327 23	....	2,266,058 67	10,013,808 37	1.18	40.63	10.96	48.41
$6,192,761 94	$3,781,113 48	$10,802,776 53	$23,891,445 25	20.02	90.15	3.07	6.78
$169,420 40	....	$296,392 60	$5,841,260 69	3.79	90.81	.44	8.75
187,315 73	....	197,376 96	150,628 17	.19	89.35	6.04	4.61
214,714 17	$73,410 62	290,268 99	652,965 65	.16	66.81	10.21	22.98
251,859 34	....	254,687 54	1,269,771 11	.14	36.21	10.66	53.13
$823,309 64	$73,410 62	$1,038,726 09	$7,914,625 62	4.28	88.12	1.38	10.50
160,640 78	....	$196,902 02	$1,144,790 53	.90	91.54	1.25	7.21
11,486 44	....	15,506 59	18,233 80	.04	94.69	2.44	2.87
34,946 27	....	35,273 65	241,313 27	.03	52.77	6.02	41.21
29,258 70	....	31,672 88	634,781 42	.07	48.79	2.43	48.78
$236,332 19	....	$279,355 14	$2,039,119 02	1.04	87.39	1.53	11.08

regarding this see section of main report under the heading "Personal Taxes."

TABLE

SUMMARY—*Tax Levies,* 1899 *to* 1914, *Including Real Estate (Lands and Buildings), lections from October* 2, 1899, *to December* 31, 1914, *Together with Overpayments, gated According to Year of Levy.*

Year of Levy.	Amount of Levy.	Collections. Total.	Collections. Less Refunds and Over and Double Payments.	Collections. Net.	Discounts.
1899....	$86,180,076 53	$80,226,357 98	$252,422 29	$79,973,935 69	$424,437 25
1900....	82,539,201 95	76,225,126 85	160,880 88	76,064,245 97	424,772 25
1901....	88,241,801 86	79,697,884 22	475,532 31	79,222,351 91	409,295 42
1902....	88,228,554 92	79,431,042 09	171,752 06	79,259,290 03	428,928 54
1903....	77,631,774 55	71,066,269 58	130,461 57	70,935,808 01	398,559 61
1904....	86,068,403 50	79,412,480 97	221,645 08	79,190,835 89	481,195 69
1905....	88,980,686 02	80,888,774 74	333,259 33	80,555,515 41	513,077 42
1906....	94,095,093 41	86,895,687 69	257,983 90	86,637,703 79	526,352 65
1907....	101,947,670 02	93,948,288 39	502,464 92	93,445,823 47	489,832 80
1908....	116,541,083 61	109,301,249 35	490,807 72	108,810,441 63	....
1909....	122,742,633 66	115,668,030 22	357,087 63	115,310,942 59	....
1910....	131,474,769 92	124,365,687 12	402,827 72	123,962,859 40	....
1911....	142,237,759 37	134,589,172 44	203,907 89	134,385,264 55	....
1912....	150,956,705 75	142,452,335 34	146,526 19	142,305,809 15	317,518 77
1913....	151,786,268 41	139,630,518 98	117,046 01	139,513,472 97	278,930 07
1914....	150,503,514 53	124,411,584 72	44,671 04	124,366,913 68	292,101 90
	$1,760,155,998 01	$1,618,210,490 68	$4,269,276 54	$1,613,941,214 14	$4,985,002 37

TABLE

REAL ESTATE (LANDS AND BUILDINGS) *Levies* 1899 *to* 1914. *Inclusive, Overpayments, Discounts, Cancellations Thereon Segregated*

Year of Action.	Amount of Levy.	Collections. Total.	Collections. Less Refunds and Over and Double Payments.
1899......................	$70,422,015 41	$56,058,661 33	....
1900......................	66,109,359 06	61,550,676 22	$51,527 42
1901......................	69,985,905 58	66,892,351 39	49,508 11
1902......................	70,550,043 48	69,881,334 74	77,558 15
1903......................	64,149,021 06	64,801,914 87	72,302 08
1904......................	72,220,078 07	71.245,531 50	94,571 63
1905......................	73,585,830 65	74,295,276 86	154,114 76
1906......................	79,496,876 72	77,490,442 45	131,279 68
1907......................	85.580,422 29	78.051,541 53	104,260 33
1908......................	99,989,581 80	96,243,108 38	180,874 54
1909......................	105.933,728 87	105,560,202 85	351.144 31
1910......................	115,080,167 28	111,498,048 03	236,395 80
1911......................	124,845.014 59	121.735,760 78	187,230 52
1912......................	133,946,733 95	135,581.104 34	124,421 81
1913......................	134,590,929 55	134,156,935 28	232.055 42
1914......................	133,831,562 06	131,626,864 80	173,903 74
	$1.500,317,270 42	$1,456,670.355 35	$2,221,148 30

B.

Real Estate of Corporations, Special Franchise and Personal Taxes, Showing Col- Discounts, Cancellations and Deductions Under Section 48 of the Tax Law, Segre-

Cancellations.	Deductions Under Section 48, Tax Law.	Total.	Balance Uncollected at December 31, 1914.	Percentages. Net Collections to Levy.	Total Discounts, Cancellations and Deductions to Levy.	Un-Collected Balance to Levy.
$1,194,279 01	....	$1,618,716 26	$4,587,424 58	92.80	1.88	5.32
2,733,083 40	$274,482 05	3,432,337 70	3,042,618 28	92.14	4.16	3.70
3,403,388 25	550,908 44	4,363,592 11	4,655,857 84	89.78	4.94	5.28
3,543,803 70	565,382 21	4,538,114 45	4,431,150 44	89.84	5.14	5.02
1,693,461 58	539,940 30	2,631,961 49	4,064,005 05	91.37	3.39	5.24
1,240,677 89	560,684 08	2,282,557 66	4,595,009 95	92.01	2.65	5.34
2,463,996 56	599,032 55	3,576,106 53	4,849,064 08	90.53	4.02	5.45
2,598,524 83	648,013 68	3,772,891 16	3,684,498 46	92.08	4.00	3.92
3,440,428 10	756,770 40	4,687,031 30	3,814,815 25	91.66	4.60	3.74
3,646,781 27	880,772 34	4,527,553 61	3,203,088 37	93.37	3.88	2:75
3,218,646 27	982,870 12	4,201,516 39	3,230,174 68	93.95	3.42	2.63
2,115,711 04	928,992 43	3,044,703 47	4,467,207 05	94.29	2.31	3.40
1,669,919 41	979,360 45	2,649,279 86	5,203,214 96	94.48	1.86	3.66
919,791 01	647,361 39	1,884,671 17	6,766,225 43	94.27	1.25	4.48
306,296 53	967,928 91	1,553,155 51	10,719,639 93	91.92	1.02	7.06
166,626 47	968,765 45	1,427,493 82	24,709,107 03	82.64	.95	16.41
$34,355,415 32	$10,851,264 80	$50,191,682 49	$96,023,101 38	91.70	2.85	5.45

C.

Showing Collections from October 2, 1899, to December 31, 1914, Together with According to Year in Which Transactions Occurred.

Net.	Discounts.	Cancellations.		Total.
$56,058,661 33	$366,284 13	....	....	$366,284 13
61,499,148 80	366,631 89	$66,140 77	....	432,772 66
66,842,843 28	362,974 93	70,371 54	....	433,346 47
69,803,776 59	384,775 78	233,734 44	....	618,510 22
64,729,612 79	361,537 66	179,517 48	....	541,055 14
71,150,959 87	440,272 45	167,649 36	....	607,921 81
74,141,162 10	468,956 39	184,775 77	....	653,732 16
77,359,162 77	489,633 26	219,241 84	....	708,875 10
77,947,281 20	448,939 83	224,690 77	....	673,630 60
96,062,233 84	39 68	370,780 45	....	370,820 13
105,209,058 54	....	528,010 13	....	528,010 13
111,261,652 23	....	290,587 61	....	290,587 61
121,548,530 26	....	376,067 81	....	376,067 81
135,457,282 53	285,499 85	393,887 01	....	679,386 86
133,974,879 86	258,375 89	559,789 69	....	818,165 58
131,452,961 06	264,898 32	1,222,417 33	....	1,487,315 65
$1,454,449,207 05	$4,498,820 06	$5,087,662 00	....	$9,586,482 06

The uncollected balance on December 31, 1914, was $36,281,581.31.

TABLE

REAL ESTATE OF CORPORATIONS—*Tax Levies of* 1899 *to* 1914, *Inclusive, Overpayments, Discounts, and Cancellations Thereon,*

Year of Action.	Amount of Levy.	Collections.	
		Total.	Less Refunds and Over and Double Payments.
1899	$2,383,822 75	$976,059 89	$0 40
1900	679,268 62	617,961 84	....
1901	721,067 36	434,784 35	22,791 24
1902	704,173 61	517,057 07	38,557 59
1903	418,359 13	1,004,868 95	26,939 48
1904	495,012 08	520,147 47	11,276 21
1905	493,042 26	476,867 38	1,932 51
1906	759,212 75	525,619 42	15,248 25
1907	1,048,897 83	561,821 64	472 40
1908	1,445,418 58	944,208 98	35,408 91
1909	1,289,192 17	1,016,615 28	8,312 46
1910	1,555,696 39	1,153,315 06	1,953 52
1911	2,881,065 74	2,531,145 22	1 00
1912	3,109,931 58	2,605,101 14	44 54
1913	3,290,268 45	3,410,747 10	944 77
1914	3,339,684 26	3,076,849 08	28 51
Total	$24,614,113 56	$20,373,169 87	$163,911 79

TABLE

SPECIAL FRANCHISE TAXES—*Levies of* 1900 *to* 1914, *Inclusive, Showing Discounts, Cancellations, and Deductions Under Section* 48 *of the Tax*

Year of Action.	Amount of Levy.	Collections.	
		Total.	Less Refunds and Over and Double Payments.
1900	$4,969,748 58	$15,101 51	....
1901	4,925,291 84	211,574 46	$1,653 33
1902	5,049,106 47	158,952 88	....
1903	3,360,543 42	152,197 19	22 34
1904	3,837,072 69	384,083 42	15,094 63
1905	4,546,986 43	6,005,121 83	11,215 88
1906	5,394,041 11	1,025,994 51	75,076 36
1907	7,005,982 97	3,328,808 81	9,027 04
1908	8,017,257 50	1,937,167 62	17,353 41
1909	8,022,692 92	5,725,907 27	7,018 00
1910	8,249,097 11	12,710,612 32	308,696 16
1911	8,325,934 55	8,125,303 78	675,068 60
1912	7,602,095 49	6,756,782 93	292,448 13
1913	7,991,775 16	6,960,625 38	79,460 61
1914	7,248,956 94	4,191,741 66	4,528 74
Total	$94,546,583 16	$57,689,975 57	$1,496,663 23

D.

Showing Collections from October 2, 1899, to December 31, 1914, Together With Segregated According to Year in Which Transactions Occurred.

Net.	Discounts.	Cancellations.		Total.
$976,059 49	$5,091 17	....	....	$5,091 17
617,961 84	2,573 88	....	....	2,573 88
411,993 11	3,744 61	$1,188 87	....	4,933 48
478,499 48	3,983 96	23,226 25	....	27,210 21
977,929 47	3,335 74	352,232 52	....	355,568 26
508,871 26	3,611 56	1,200 93	....	4,812 49
474,934 87	3,985 53	46,441 68	....	50,427 21
510,371 17	4,176 80	511,445 18	....	515,621 98
561,349 24	4,892 06	27,568 45	....	32,460 51
908,800 07	....	167,836 34	....	167,836 34
1,008,302 82	....	472,099 44	....	472,099 44
1,151,361 54	....	105,590 17	....	105,590 17
2,531,144 22	....	130,371 39	....	130,371 39
2,605,056 60	12,779 61	698,343 02	....	711,122 63
3,409,802 33	5,955 66	129,551 01	....	135,506 67
3,076,820 57	9,493 65	665,895 33	....	675,388 98
$20,209,258 08	$63,624 23	$3,332,990 58	....	$3,396,614 81

The uncollected balance on December 31, 1914, was $1,008,240.67.

E.

Collections from October 1, 1900, to December 31, 1914, Together with Overpayments, Law, Segregated According to Year in Which Transactions Occurred.

Net.	Discounts.	Cancellations.	Deductions Under Section 48, Tax Law.	Total.
$15,101 51	$134 25	....	....	$134 25
209,921 13	61 34	$103,563 23	....	103,624 57
158,952 88	130 23	69,247 07	....	69,377 30
152,174 85	1,091 56	991,785 17	....	992,876 73
368,988 79	1,765 40	54,875 91	....	56,641 31
5,993,905 95	3,837 73	398,608 01	....	402,445 74
950,918 15	873 88	354,635 02	....	355,508 90
3,319,781 77	6,527 13	1,417,555 47	....	1,424,082 60
1,919,814 21	....	26,272 85	$199,351 20	225,624 05
5,718,889 27	....	1,598,149 50	4,814,700 73	6,412,850 23
12,401,916 16	....	4,331,139 64	1,137,393 13	5,468,532 77
7,450,235 18	....	3,631,802 11	1,521,377 38	5,153,179 49
6,464,334 80	19,239 31	1,998,317 63	997,463 10	3,015,020 04
6,881,164 77	14,594 07	1,040,897 12	1,209,364 72	2,264,855 91
4,187,212 92	17,714 38	351,127 32	971,614 54	1,340,456 24
$56,193,312 34	$65,969 28	$16,367,976 05	$10,851,264 80	$27,285,210 13

The uncollected balance on December 31, 1914, was $11,068,060.69.

TABLE

PERSONAL PROPERTY TAXES—*Levies,* 1899 *to* 1914, *Inclusive, Showing ments, Discounts and Cancellations Thereon, Segregated*

Year of Action.	Amount of Levy.	Collections. Total.	Collections. Less Refunds and Over and Double Payments.
1899	$13,374,238 37	$7,345,236 47	$2,685 43
1900	10,780,825 69	7,478,571 97	19,251 15
1901	12,609,537 08	6,823,895 57	65,183 28
1902	11,925,231 36	6,793,023 50	14,628 04
1903	9,703,850 94	5,272,533 87	163,076 76
1904	9,516,240 66	5,096,515 77	2,433 33
1905	10,354,826 68	4,952,470 09	98,830 61
1906	8,444,962 83	4,335,584 55	5,199 61
1907	8,312,366 93	4,449,381 91	1,011 15
1908	7,088,825 73	4,428,397 13	677 46
1909	7,497,019 70	4,629,831 86	1,873 61
1910	6,589,809 14	4,883,300 87	2,773 98
1911	6,185,744 49	4,416,294 55	3,453 75
1912	6,297,944 75	4,508,551 27	2,433 11
1913	5,913,295 25	3,998,440 81	2,024 38
1914	6,083,311 27	4,064,959 70	2,017 57
	$140,678,030 87	$83,476,989 89	$387,553 22

TABLE

RECAPITULATION—Real Estate (Lands and Buildings), Real Estate of Corpora Collections from October 2, 1899, *to December* 31, 1914, *Together With Tax Law, Segregated According to Year in Which Transactions Occurred.*

Year of Action.	Amount of Levy.	Collections. Total.	Collections. Less Refunds and Over and Double Payments.
1899	$86,180,076 53	$64,379,957 69	$2,685 83
1900	82,539,201 95	69,662,311 54	70,778 57
1901	88,241,801 86	74,362,605 77	139,135 96
1902	88,228,554 92	77,350,368 19	130,743 78
1903	77,631,774 55	71,231,514 88	262,340 66
1904	86,068,403 50	77,246,278 16	123,375 80
1905	88,980,686 02	85,729,736 16	266,093 76
1906	94,095,093 41	83,377,640 93	226,803 90
1907	101,947,670 02	86,391,553 89	114,770 92
1908	116,541,083 61	103,552,882 11	234,314 32
1909	122,742,633 66	116,932,557 26	368,348 38
1910	131,474,769 92	130,245,276 28	549,819 46
1911	142,237,759 37	136,808,504 33	865,753 87
1912	150,956,705 75	149,452,139 68	419,347 59
1913	151,786,268 41	148,526,748 57	314,485 18
1914	150,503,514 53	142,960,415 24	180,478 56
	$1,760,155,998 01	$1,618,210,490 68	$4,269,276 54

F.

Collections from October 2, 1899, to December 31, 1914, Together with Overpay-According to Year in Which Transactions Occurred.

Net.	Discounts.	Cancellations.		Total.
$7,342,551 04	$53,061 95	....	....	$53,061 95
7,459,320 82	55,432 23	$32,031 51	....	87,463 74
6,758,712 29	42,499 93	36,538 43	....	79,038 36
6,778,395 46	40,053 18	326,084 66	....	366,137 84
5,109,457 11	32,553 28	771,340 35	....	803,893 63
5,094,082 44	35,587 65	1,541,403 27	....	1,576,990 92
4,853,639 48	36,297 77	733,630 47	....	769,928 24
4,330,384 94	31,668 71	549,868 30	....	581,537 01
4,448,370 76	29,434 10	1,249,950 93	....	1,279,385 03
4,427,719 67	....	545,117 75	....	545,117 75
4,627,958 25	....	452,556 66	....	452,556 66
4,880,526 89	....	690,780 63	....	690,780 63
4,412,840 80	....	357,999 80	....	357,999 80
4,506,118 16	....	604,284 32	....	604,284 32
3,996,416 43	....	1,023,968 38	....	1,023,968 38
4,062,942 13	....	651,231 23	....	651,231 23
$83.089,436 67	$356,588 80	$9,566,786 69	....	$9,923,375 49

The uncollected balance on December 31, 1914, was $47,665,218.71 of which approx imately $45,000,000 is uncollectible.

G.

tions, Special Franchise and Personal Taxes Levied 1899 to 1914 Inclusive, Showing Overpayments, Discounts, Cancellations and Deductions Under Section 48 of the

Net.	Discounts.	Cancellations.	Deductions Under Section 48, Tax Law.	Total.
$64,377,271 86	$424,437 25	....	....	$424,437 25
69,591,532 97	424,772 25	$98,172 28	....	522,944 53
74,223,469 81	409,280 81	211,662 07	....	620,942 88
77,219,624 41	428,943 15	652,292 42	....	1,081,235 57
70,969,174 22	398,518 24	2,294,875 52	....	2,693,393 76
77,122,902 36	481,237 06	1,765,129 47	....	2,246,366 53
85,463,642 40	513,077 42	1,363,455 93	....	1,876,533 35
83,150,837 03	526,352 65	1,635,190 34	....	2,161,542 99
86,276,782 97	489,793 12	2,919,765 62	....	3,409,558 74
103,318,567 79	39 68	1,110,007 39	$199,351 20	1,309,398 27
116,564,208 88	....	3,050,815 73	4,814,700 73	7,865,516 46
129,695,456 82	....	5,418,098 05	1,137,393 13	6,555,491 18
135,942,750 46	....	4,496,241 11	1,521,377 38	6,017,618 49
149,032,792 09	317,518 77	3,694,831 98	997,463 10	5,009,813 85
148,212,263 39	278,925 62	2,754,206 20	1,209,364 72	4,242,496 54
142,779,936 68	292,106 35	2,890,671 21	971,614 54	4,154,392 10
$1,613,941,214 14	$4,985,002 37	$34,355,415 32	$10,851,264 80	$50,191,682 49

TABLE I.—TAX

	Amount of Levy.	Collections. Total.	Collections. Less Refunds and Over and Double Payments.	Collections. Net.	Discounts.
		Part I.—Classified According to General			
Real Estate (Lands and Buildings)	$70,422,015 41	$69,720,735 59	$178,802 19	$69,541,933 40	$366,284 13
Real Estate of Corporations	2,383,822 75	2,000,118 30	50,226 46	1,949,891 84	5,091 17
Personal Property	13,374,238 37	8,505,504 09	23,393 64	8,482,110 45	53,061 95
Grand Totals	$86,180,076 53	$80,226,357 98	$252,422 29	$79,973,935 69	$424,437 25
		Part II.—Classified			
Manhattan	$62,814,741 81	$58,040,807 19	$180,737 57	$57,860,069 62	$325,107 33
The Bronx	3,236,607 56	3,082,039 85	5,980 47	3,076,059 38	13,219 68
Brooklyn	15,459,721 79	14,804,795 71	54,594 49	14,750,201 22	70,725 55
Queens	3,600,792 88	3,315,830 31	7,960 57	3,307,869 74	11,125 63
Richmond	1,068,212 49	982,884 92	3,149 19	979,735 73	4,259 06
Grand Totals	$86,180,076 53	$80,226,357 98	$252,422 29	$79,973,935 69	$424,437 25
		Part III.—Classified According to Boroughs			
Manhattan.					
Real Estate (Lands and Buildings)	$49,641,685 44	$49,220,278 41	$140,074 43	$49,080,203 98	$274,246 09
Real Estate of Corporations	1,327,759 26	1,150,210 91	17,362 80	1,132,848 11	1,700 40
Personal Property	11,845,297 11	7,670,317 87	23,300 34	7,647,017 53	49,160 84
Totals	$62,814,741 81	$58,040,807 19	$180,737 57	$57,860,069 62	$325,107 33
The Bronx.					
Real Estate (Lands and Buildings)	$2,816,829 07	$2,785,517 95	$5,796 52	$2,779,721 43	$11,172 63
Real Estate of Corporations	251,311 61	236,328 86	159 15	236,169 71	1,732 86
Personal Property	168,466 88	60,193 04	24 80	60,168 24	314 19
Totals	$3,236,607 56	$3,082,039 85	$5,980 47	$3,076,059 38	$13,219 68
Brooklyn.					
Real Estate (Lands and Buildings)	$13,887,222 23	$13,808,545 41	$21,821 48	$13,786,723 93	$66,950 10
Real Estate of Corporations	508,381 77	373,217 07	32,704 51	340,512 56	924 06
Personal Property	1,064,117 79	623,033 23	68 50	622,964 73	2,851 39
Totals	$15,459,721 79	$14,804,795 71	$54,594 49	$14,750,201 22	$70,725 55
Queens.					
Real Estate (Lands and Buildings)	$3,172,151 96	$3,040,285 77	$7,960 57	$3,032,325 20	$10,407 30
Real Estate of Corporations	224,676 24	176,974 72	....	176,974 72	303 84
Personal Property	203,964 68	98,569 82	....	98,569 82	414 49
Totals	$3,600,792 88	$3,315,830 31	$7,960 57	$3,307,869 74	$11,125 63
Richmond.					
Real Estate (Lands and Buildings)	$904,126 71	$866,108 05	$3,149 19	$862,958 86	$3,508 01
Real Estate of Corporations	71,693 87	63,386 74	....	63,386 74	430 01
Personal Property	92,391 91	53,390 13	....	53,390 13	321 04
Totals	$1,068,212 49	$982,884 92	$3,149 19	$979,735 73	$4,259 06

LEVY OF 1899.

Cancellations.		Total.	Balance Uncollected at Dec. 31, 1914.	Percentages. Borough and Specific Levy to Total Levy.	Net Collections to Levy.	Total Discounts, Cancellations and Deductions to Levy.	Uncollected Balance to Levy.
Character of Taxable Property.							
$323,316 21	....	$689,600 34	$190,481 67	81.72	98.75	.97	.28
417,843 84	....	422,935 01	10,995 90	2.76	81.80	17.74	.46
453,118 96	....	506,180 91	4,385,947 01	15.52	63.43	3.78	32.79
$1,194,279 01	....	$1,618,716 26	$4,587,424 58	100.00	92.80	1.88	5.32
According to Boroughs.							
$834,066 06	....	$1,159,173 39	$3,795,498 80	72.89	92.11	1.85	6.04
28,405 65	....	41,625 33	118,922 85	3.75	95.04	1.29	3.67
197,544 62	....	268,270 17	441,250 40	17.94	95.41	1.74	2.85
100,874 73	....	112,000 36	180,922 78	4.18	91.87	3.11	5.02
33,387 95	....	37,647 01	50,829 75	1.24	91.72	3.52	4.76
$1,194,279 01	....	$1,618,716 26	$4,587,424 58	100.00	92.80	1.88	5.32
and General Character of Taxable Property.							
$218,198 88	....	$492,444 97	$69,036 49	57.62	98.87	.99	.14
193,099 14	....	194,799 54	111 61	1.53	85.32	14.67	.01
422,768 04	....	471,928 88	3,726,350 70	13.74	64.56	3.98	31.46
$834,066 06	....	$1,159,173 39	$3,795,498 80	72.89	92.11	1.85	6.04
$13,981 73	....	$25,154 36	$11,953 28	3.27	98.68	.89	.43
13,404 08	....	15,136 94	4 96	.29	93.98	6.02	....
1,019 84	....	1,334 03	106,964 61	.19	35.71	.80	63.49
$28,405 65	....	$41,625 33	$118,922 85	3.75	95.04	1.29	3.67
$19,243 92	....	$86,194 02	$14,304 28	16.12	99.28	.62	.10
166,775 30	....	167,699 36	169 85	.59	66.98	32.99	.03
11,525 40	....	14,376 79	426,776 27	1.23	58.54	1.35	40.11
$197,544 62	....	$268,270 17	$441,250 40	17.94	95.41	1.74	2.85
$38,827 29	....	$49,234 59	$90,592 17	3.68	95.59	1.56	2.85
44,565 32	....	44,869 16	2,832 36	.26	78.77	19.97	1.26
17,482 12	....	17,896 61	87,498 25	.24	48.33	8.78	42.89
$100,874 73	....	$112,000 36	$180,922 78	4.18	91.87	3.11	5.02
$33,064 39	....	$36,572 40	$4,595 45	1.05	95.44	4.05	.51
....	....	430 01	7,877 12	.08	88.41	.60	10.99
323 56	....	644 60	38,357 18	.11	57.79	.70	41.51
$33,387 95	....	$37,647 01	$50,829 75	1.24	91.72	3.52	4.76

Part I-A—Tax Levy of 1899, Supporting and Amplifying Totals Shown in Part I of Classified According to General Character of Taxable Property and

Class of Tax and Year of Action.	Amount of Levy.	Collections. Total.	Collections. Less Refunds and Over and Double Payments.	Collections. Net.	Discounts.
Real Estate (Lands and Buildings)—					
1899.........	$70,422,015 41	$56,058,661 33	....	$56,058,661 33	$366,284 13
1900.........	....	8,475,099 56	$51,527 42	8,423,572 14	....
1901.........	....	2,237,598 51	15,860 39	2,221,738 12	....
1902.........	....	1,172,716 88	13,132 44	1,159,584 44	....
1903.........	....	479,078 58	2,800 19	476,278 39	....
1904.........	....	395,113 91	15,499 94	379,613 97	....
1905.........	....	430,871 91	20,856 57	410,015 34	....
1906.........	....	143,219 49	24,837 69	118,381 80	....
1907.........	....	101,486 98	900 42	100,586 56	....
1908.........	....	50,465 10	3,027 66	47,437 44	....
1909.........	....	63,696 52	26,207 89	37,488 63	....
1910.........	....	44,432 52	127 73	44,304 79	....
1911.........	....	25,785 14	1,414 74	24,370 40	....
1912.........	....	22,865 40	731 48	22,133 92	....
1913.........	....	12,423 11	967 30	11,455 81	....
1914.........	....	7,220 65	910 33	6,310 32	....
Total....	$70,422,015 41	$69,720,735 59	$178,802 19	$69,541,933 40	$366,284 13
Real Estate of Corporations—					
1899.........	$2,383,822 75	$976,059 89	$0 40	$976,059 49	$5,091 17
1900.........	....	319,816 13	....	319,816 13	....
1901.........	....	6,874 24	....	6,874 24	....
1902.........	....	48,400 13	....	48,400 13	....
1903.........	....	537,833 04	19,760 49	518,072 55	....
1904.........	....	215 09	....	215 09	....
1905.........	....	22,397 23	....	22,397 23	....
1906.........	....	2,364 24	....	2,364 24	....
1907.........	....	6,771 60	106 39	6,665 21	....
1908.........	....	61,083 44	30,359 18	30,724 26	....
1909.........	....	12,640 32	....	12,640 32	....
1910.........	....	661 99	....	661 99	....
1911.........	....	884 10	....	884 10	....
1912.........	....	709 26	....	709 26	....
1913.........	....	12 40	....	12 40	....
1914.........	....	3,395 20	....	3,395 20	....
Total....	$2,383,822 75	$2,000,118 30	$50,226 46	$1,949,891 84	$5,091 17
Personal Property—					
1899.........	$13,374,238 37	$7,345,236 47	$2,685 43	$7,342,551 04	$53,061 95
1900.........	....	784,902 11	15,412 47	769,489 64	....
1901.........	....	161,148 32	5,223 56	155,924 76	....
1902.........	....	143,393 95	....	143,393 95	....
1903.........	....	29,237 01	47 38	29,189 63	....
1904.........	....	11,498 27	24 80	11,473 47	....
1905.........	....	21,935 22	....	21,935 22	....
1906.........	....	838 03	....	838 03	....
1907.........	....	946 72	....	946 72	....
1908.........	....	1,792 23	....	1,792 23	....

Table 1, Showing All Transactions from October 2, 1899, to December 31, 1914, Further Analyzed According to Year in Which Transactions Were Made.

Cancellations.		Total.	Balance Uncollected at December 31, 1914.	Percentages.		
				Net Collections to Levy.	Total Discounts, Cancellations and Deductions to Levy.	Un-Collected Balance to Levy.
....	....	$366,284 13	....	....	....	....
$62,849 46	....	62,849 46	....	....	....	....
45,544 65	....	45,544 65	....	....	....	....
14,997 57	....	14,997 57	....	....	....	....
21,349 01	....	21,349 01	....	....	....	....
23,620 85	....	23,620 85	....	....	....	....
26,384 01	....	26,384 01	....	....	....	....
32,514 92	....	32,514 92	....	....	....	....
1,694 35	....	1,694 35	....	....	....	....
8,393 21	....	8,393 21	....	....	....	....
27,800 46	....	27,800 46	....	....	....	....
6,402 21	....	6,402 21	....	....	....	....
862 70	....	862 70	....	....	....	....
1,984 82	....	1,984 82	....	....	....	....
1,758 11	....	1,758 11	....	....	....	....
47,159 88	....	47,159 88	....	....	....	....
$323,316 21	....	$689,600 34	$190,481 67	98.75	.97	.28
....	....	$5,091 17	....	....	....	....
....	....	....	....	....	....	....
....	....	....	....	....	....	....
$3,546 36	....	3,546 36	....	....	....	....
231,721 95	....	231,721 95	....	....	....	....
158 75	....	158 75	....	....	....	....
12,402 00	....	12,402 00	....	....	....	....
4,960 80	....	4,960 80	....	....	....	....
....	....	....	....	....	....	....
156,140 80	....	156,140 80	....	....	....	....
....	....	....	....	....	....	....
....	....	....	....	....	....	....
8,913 18	....	8,913 18	....	....	....	....
....	....	....	....	....	....	....
....	....	....	....	....	....	....
....	....	....	....	....	....	....
$417,843 84	....	$422,935 01	$10,995 90	81.80	17.74	.46
....	....	$53,061 95	....	....	....	....
$31,226 69	....	31,226 69	....	....	....	....
12,771 92	....	12,771 92	....	....	....	....
89,504 16	....	89,504 16	....	....	....	....
29,529 98	....	29,529 98	....	....	....	....
266,762 40	....	266,762 40	....	....	....	....
16,289 69	....	16,289 69	....	....	....	....
60 08	....	60 08	....	....	....	....
1,004 56	....	1,004 56	....	....	....	......
4,408 26	....	4,408 26	....	....	....	....

Class of Tax and Year of Action.	Amount of Levy.	Collections. Total.	Collections. Less Refunds and Over and Double Payments.	Collections. Net.	Discounts.
Personal Property—					
1909.........	....	209 24	....	209 24	....
1910.........	....	1,193 07	....	1,193 07	....
1911.........	....	118 21	....	118 21	....
1912.........	....	70 89	....	70 89	....
1913.........	....	411 76	....	411 76	....
1914.........	....	2,572 59	....	2,572 59	....
Total	$13,374,238 37	$8,505,504 09	$23,393 64	$8,482,110 45	$53,061 95

Part I-B—Recapitulation—Combining the Three Classes of Tax Shown in the Pre
According to the Ye

Totals for—					
1899.........	$86,180,076 53	$64,379,957 69	$2,685 83	$64,377,271 86	$424,437 25
1900.........	....	9,579,817 80	66,939 89	9,512,877 91	....
1901.........	....	2,405,621 07	21,083 95	2,384,537 12	....
1902.........	....	1,364,510 96	13,132 44	1,351,378 52	....
1903.........	....	1,046,148 63	22,608 06	1,023,540 57	....
1904.........	....	406,827 27	15,524 74	391,302 53	....
1905.........	....	475,204 36	20,856 57	454,347 79	....
1906.........	....	146,421 76	24,837 69	121,584 07	....
1907.........	....	109,205 30	1,006 81	108,198 49	....
1908.........	....	113,340 77	33,386 84	79,953 93	....
1909.........	....	76,546 08	26,207 89	50,338 19	....
1910.........	....	46,287 58	127 73	46,159 85	....
1911.........	....	26,787 45	1,414 74	25,372 71	....
1912.........	....	23,645 55	731 48	22,914 07	....
1913.........	....	12,847 27	967 30	11,879 97	....
1914.........	....	13,188 44	910 33	12,278 11	....
Grand Totals..	$86,180,076 53	$80,226,357 98	$252,422 29	$79,973,935 69	$424,437 25

TABLE II.—TAX

	Amount of Levy.	Collections. Total.	Collections. Less Refunds and Over and Double Payments.	Collections. Net.	Discounts.
			Part I.—Classified	*According*	*to General*
Real Estate (Lands and Buildings)	$66,109,359 06	$65,434,931 05	$100,381 39	$65,334,549 66	$366,631 89
Real Estate of Corporations..	679,268 62	461,394 72	4,795 42	456,599 30	2,573 88
Special Franchise	4,969,748 58	2,704,328 08	28,073 07	2,676,255 01	134 25
Personal Property	10,780,825 69	7,624,473 00	27,631 00	7,596,842 00	55,432 23
Grand Totals........	$82,539,201 95	$76,225,126 85	$160,880 88	$76,064,245 97	$424,772 25
				Part II.—	*Classified*
Manhattan	$59,480,217 38	$54,846,983 47	$129,367 24	$54,717,616 23	$326,905 99
The Bronx	3,292,556 14	3,070,778 02	6,967 22	3,063,810 80	13,262 47
Brooklyn	16,106,204 46	14,967,949 25	18,281 00	14,949,668 25	71,328 73
Queens	2,572,863 66	2,400,900 49	3,710 94	2,397,189 55	9,139 27
Richmond	1,087,360 31	938,515 62	2,554 48	935,961 14	4,135 79
Grand Totals........	$82,539,201 95	$76,225,126 85	$160,880 88	$76,064,245 97	$424,772 25

Cancellations.		Total.	Balance Uncollected at December 31, 1914.	Percentages. Net Collections to Levy.	Total Discounts, Cancellations and Deductions to Levy.	Un-Collected Balance to Levy.
....	....	....	....	....	....	....
....	....	....	....	....	....	....
....	....	....	....	....	....	....
130 60	....	130 60	....	....	....	....
1,430 62	....	1,430 62	....	....	....	....
....	....	....	....	....	....	....
$453,118 96	....	$506,180 91	$4,385,947 01	63.43	3.78	32.79

ceding Part (I-A) and Summarizing the Transactions of the Entire Levy of 1899 *ar of Occurrence.*

....	....	$424,437 25	....	74.70	.49	....
$94,076 15	....	94,076 15	....	11.04	.11	....
58,316 57	....	58,316 57	....	2.77	.07	....
108,048 09	....	108,048 09	....	1.57	.13	....
282,600 94	....	282,600 94	....	1.19	.33	....
290,542 00	....	290,542 00	....	.45	.34	....
55,075 70	....	55,075 70	....	.53	.06	....
37,535 80	....	37,535 80	....	.14	.04	....
2,698 91	....	2,698 91	....	.12	.00	....
168,942 27	....	168,942 27	....	.09	.20	....
27,800 46	....	27,800 46	....	.06	.03	....
6,402 21	....	6,402 21	....	.05	.01	....
9,775 88	....	9,775 88	....	.03	.01	....
2,115 42	....	2,115 42	....	.03	.00	....
3,188 73	....	3,188 73	....	.01	.00	....
47,159 88	....	47,159 88	....	.02	.06	....
$1,194,279 01	....	$1,618,716 26	$4,587,424 58	92.80	1.88	5.32

Levy of 1900.

Cancellations.	Deductions Under Section 48, Tax Law.	Total.	Balance Uncollected at Dec. 31, 1914.	Percentages. Borough and Specific Levy to Total Levy.	Net Collections to Levy.	Total Discounts, Cancellations and Deductions to Levy.	Un-collected Balance to Levy.
Character of Taxable Property.							
$286,030 40	....	$652,662 29	$122,147 11	80.10	98.83	.99	.18
210,796 73	....	213,370 61	9,298 71	.82	67.23	31.41	1.36
1,753,691 32	$274,482 05	2,028,307 62	265,185 95	6.02	53.85	40.82	5.33
482,564 95	....	537,997 18	2,645.986 51	13.06	70.47	4.99	24.54
$2,733,083 40	$274,482 05	$3,432,337 70	$3,042,618 28	100.00	92.16	4.16	3.68
According to Boroughs.							
$2,077,057 55	$91,535 64	$2,495,499 18	$2,267,101 97	72.06	91.99	4.20	3.81
66,908 68	....	80,171 15	148,574 19	3.99	93.05	2.44	4.51
486,018 98	182,946 41	740,294 12	416,242 09	19.51	92.82	4.60	2.58
60,023 57	....	69,162 84	106,511 27	3.12	93.17	2.69	4.14
43,074 62	....	47,210 41	104,188 76	1.32	86.08	4.34	9.58
$2,733,083 40	$274,482 05	$3,432,337 70	$3,042,618 28	100.00	92.16	4.16	3.68

Part III.—Classified According to Boroughs

	Amount of Levy.	Collections. Total.	Collections. Less Refunds and Over and Double Payments.	Collections. Net.	Discounts.
Manhattan.					
Real Estate (Lands and Buildings)	$46,161,675 70	$45,767,495 90	$75,409 31	$45,692,086 59	$275,531 30
Real Estate of Corporations..	247,121 96	83,987 27	4,495 42	79,491 85	47 69
Special Franchise	3,748,363 22	2,130,429 84	22,320 87	2,108,108 97	12 06
Personal Property	9,323,056 50	6,865,070 46	27,141 64	6,837,928 82	51,314 94
Totals	$59,480,217 38	$54,846,983 47	$129,367 24	$54,717,616 23	$326,905 99
The Bronx.					
Real Estate (Lands and Buildings)	$2,773,232 88	$2,740,428 30	$4,224 73	$2,736,203 57	$11,414 37
Real Estate of Corporations..	176,033 79	172,518 47	195 55	172,322 92	1,554 22
Special Franchise	163,458 93	106,492 28	2,524 47	103,967 81	100 42
Personal Property	179,830 54	51,338 97	22 47	51,316 50	193 46
Totals	$3,292,556 14	$3,070,778 02	$6,967 22	$3,063,810 80	$13,262 47
Brooklyn.					
Real Estate (Lands and Buildings)	$14,064,187 44	$13,899,367 54	$14,844 31	$13,884,523 23	$67,508 02
Real Estate of Corporations..	119,114 19	92,754 23	104 45	92,649 78	505 61
Special Franchise	911,056 12	377,540 29	2,907 56	374,632 73	11 23
Personal Property	1,011,846 71	598,287 19	424 68	597,862 51	3,303 87
Totals	$16,106,204 46	$14,967,749 25	$18,281 00	$14,949,668 25	$71,328 73
Queens.					
Real Estate (Lands and Buildings)	$2,250,111 77	$2,204,092 27	$3,370 77	$2,200,721 50	$8,750 45
Real Estate of Corporations..	100,784 74	76,839 32	....	76,839 32	125 23
Special Franchise	94,548 54	70,931 22	320 17	70,611 05	10 54
Personal Property	127,418 61	49,037 68	20 00	49,017 68	253 05
Totals	$2,572,863 66	$2,400,900 49	$3,710 94	$2,397,189 55	$9,139 27
Richmond.					
Real Estate (Lands and Buildings)	$860,151 27	$823,547 04	$2,532 27	$821,014 77	$3,427 75
Real Estate of Corporations..	36,213 94	35,295 43	....	35,295 43	341 13
Special Franchise	52,321 77	18,934 45	....	18,934 45	....
Personal Property	138,673 33	60,738 70	22 21	60,716 49	366 91
Totals	$1,087,360 31	$938,515 62	$2,554 48	$935,961 14	$4,135 79

Part I-A—Tax Levy of 1900, *Supporting and Amplifying Totals Shown in Part I. Classified According to General Character of Taxable Property and Further Anal*

Class of Tax and Year of Action.	Amount of Levy.	Collections. Total.	Collections. Less Re-funds and Over and Double Payments.	Collections. Net.	Discounts.
Real Estate (Lands and Buildings)—					
1900.........	$66,109,359 06	$53,075,576 66	....	$53,075,576 66	$366,631 89
1901.........	....	8,004,781 31	$33,647 72	7,971,133 59	....
1902.........	....	2,080,924 74	8,769 81	2,072,154 93	....
1903.........	....	858,275 42	3,122 57	855,152 85	....
1904.........	....	436,804 56	8,294 92	428,509 64	....
1905.........	....	410,879 01	14,605 32	396,273 69	....
1906.........	....	156,943 14	3,176 04	153,767 10	....

Cancellations.	Deductions Under Section 48, Tax Law.	Total.	Balance Uncollected at Dec. 31, 1914.	Percentages. Borough and Specific Levy to Total Levy.	Net Collections to Levy.	Total Discounts, Cancellations and Deductions to Levy.	Uncollected Balance to Levy.
and General Character of Taxable Property.							
$143,136 62	....	$418,667 92	$50,921 19	55.93	98.98	.91	.11
167,051 99	....	167,099 68	530 43	.30	32.17	67.62	.21
1,317,485 79	$91,535 64	1,409,033 49	231,220 76	4.54	56.24	37.60	6.16
449,383 15	....	500,698 09	1,984,429 59	11.29	73.34	5.37	21.29
$2,077,057 55	$91,535 64	$2,495,499 18	$2,267,101 97	72.06	91.99	4.20	3.81
$13,284 60	....	$24,698 97	$12,330 34	3.36	98.66	.90	.44
2,083 60	....	3,637 82	73 05	.21	97.89	2.07	.04
51,232 99	....	51,333 41	8,157 71	.20	63.60	31.40	5.00
307 49	....	500 95	128,013 09	.22	28.54	.28	71.18
$66,908 68	....	$80,171 15	$148,574 19	3.99	93.05	2.44	4.51
$94,217 75	....	$161,725 77	$17,938 44	17.00	98.72	1.15	.13
17,368 96	....	17,874 57	8,589 84	.14	77.78	15.01	7.21
352,328 99	$182,946 41	535,286 63	1,136 76	1.14	41.12	58.75	.13
22,103 28	....	25,407 15	388,577 05	1.23	59.09	2.51	38.40
$486,018 98	$182,946 41	$740,294 12	$416,242 09	19.51	92.82	4.60	2.58
$5,196 39	....	$13,946 84	$35,443 43	2.73	97.81	.62	1.57
23,714 80	....	23,840 03	105 39	.12	76.24	23.66	.10
21,085 71	....	21,096 25	2,841 24	.11	74.68	22.31	3.01
10,026 67	....	10,279 72	68,121 21	.16	38.47	8.07	53.46
$60,023 57	....	$69,162 84	$106,511 27	3.12	93.17	2.69	4.14
$30,195 04	....	$33,622 79	$5,513 71	1.04	95.45	3.91	.64
577 38	....	918 51	....	.04	97.46	2.54	......
11,557 84	....	11,557 84	21,829 48	.07	36.18	22.09	41.73
744 36	....	1,111 27	76,845 57	.17	43.79	.80	55.41
$43,074 62	....	$47,210 41	$104,188 76	1.32	86.08	4.34	9.58

of Table II., Showing All Transactions from October 1, 1900, *to December* 31, 1914, *yzed According to Year in Which Transactions Were Made.*

Cancellations.	Deductions Under Section 48, Tax Law.	Total.	Balance Uncollected at December 31, 1914.	Percentages. Net Collections to Levy.	Total Discounts, Cancellations and Deductions to Levy.	Un-Collected Balance to Levy.
$3,291 31	....	$369,923 20	....	....	....	....
23,136 46	....	23,136 46	....	....	....	....
91,829 10	....	91,829 10	....	....	....	....
50,219 17	....	50,219 17	....	....	....	....
15,465 58	....	15,465 58	....	....	....	....
18,876 27	....	18,876 27	....	....	....	....
9,779 10	....	9,779 10	....	....	....	....

Class of Tax and Year of Action.	Amount of Levy.	Collections. Total.	Less Refunds and Over and Double Payments.	Net.	Discounts.
Real Estate (Lands and Buildings)—					
1907.........	....	115,879 62	7,068 87	108,810 75	....
1908.........	....	58,916 07	231 38	58,684 69	....
1909.........	....	68,021 92	14,702 87	53,319 05	....
1910.........	....	108,842 23	1,654 80	107,187 43	....
1911.........	....	26,655 06	2,443 49	24,211 57	....
1912.........	....	15,563 63	523 07	15,040 56	....
1913.........	....	9,671 11	1,530 21	8,140 90	....
1914.........	....	7,196 57	610 32	6,586 25	....
Totals...	$66,109,359 06	$65,434,931 05	$100,381 39	$65,334,549 66	$366,631 89
Real Estate of Corporations—					
1900.........	$679,268 62	$298,145 71	....	$298,145 71	$2,573 88
1901.........	....	4,897 09	$104 45	4,792 64	....
1902.........	....	9,086 53	....	9,086 53	....
1903.........	....	91,638 36	....	91,638 36	....
1904.........	....	27,745 25	195 55	27,549 70	....
1905.........	....	9,007 65	....	9,007 65	....
1906.........	....	15,046 38	4,495 42	10,550 96	....
1907.........	....	1,560 89	....	1,560 89	....
1908.........	....	1,264 76	....	1,264 76	....
1909.........	....	1,217 07	....	1,217 07	....
1910.........	....	877 69	....	877 69	....
1911.........	....	736 83	....	736 83	....
1912.........	....	46 42	....	46 42	....
1913.........	....	....	....	....	....
1914.........	....	124 09	....	124 09	....
Totals...	$679,268 62	$461,394 72	$4,795 42	$456,599 30	$2,573 88
Special Franchises—					
1900.........	$4,969,748 58	$15,101 51	....	$15,101 51	$134 25
1901.........	....	112,274 94	$1,653 33	110,621 61	....
1902.........	....	5,874 60	....	5,874 60	....
1903.........	....	23,277 88	....	23,277 88	....
1904.........	....	14,710 50	....	14,710 50	....
1905.........	....	1,970,427 53	398 52	1,970,029 01	....
1906.........	....	44,917 37	587 47	44,329 90	....
1907.........	....	204,067 75	60 68	204,007 07	....
1908.........	....	33,937 90	....	33,937 90	....
1909.........	....	119,753 73	2,884 58	116,869 15	....
1910.........	....	48,594 32	167 62	48,426 70	....
1911.........	....	98,895 93	22,320 86	76,575 07	....
1912.........	....	....	....	....	....
1913.........	....	2,982 97	....	2,982 97	....
1914.........	....	9,511 15	01	9,511 14	....
Totals...	$4,969,748 58	$2,704,328 08	$28,073 07	$2,676,255 01	$134 25
Personal Property—					
1900.........	$10,780,825 69	$6,693,669 86	$3,838 68	$6,689,831 18	$55,432 23
1901.........	....	696,651 25	23,335 29	673,315 96	....
1902.........	....	147,148 05	364 03	146,784 02	....
1903.........	....	32,981 49	70 53	32,910 96	....
1904.........	....	16,602 41	22 47	16,579 94	....

Cancellations.	Deductions Under Section 48, Tax Law.	Total.	Balance Uncollected at December 31, 1914.	Percentages. Net Collections to Levy.	Percentages. Total Discounts, Cancellations and Deductions to Levy.	Percentages. Un-Collected Balance to Levy.
7,585 82	....	7,585 82	....	....	....	....
342 42	....	342 42	....	....	....	....
16,002 55	....	16,002 55	....	....	....	....
6,221 96	....	6,221 96	....	....	....	....
1,807 65	....	1,807 65	....	....	....	....
2,218 86	....	2,218 86	....	....	....	....
2,492 51	....	2,492 51	....	....	....	....
36,761 64	....	36,761 64	....	....	....	....
$286,030 40	....	$652,662 29	$122,147 11	98.83	.98	.19
....	....	$2,573 88	....	....	....	....
$577 38	....	577 38	....	....	....	....
561 92	....	561 92	....	....	....	....
40,172 68	....	40,172 68	....	....	....	....
206 79	....	206 79	....	....	....	....
845 10	....	845 10	....	....	....	....
164,869 52	....	164,869 52	....	....	....	....
....	....	....	....	....	....	....
....	....	....	....	....	....	....
....	....	....	....	....	....	....
....	....	....	....	....	....	....
....	....	....	....	....	....	....
3,516 50	....	3,516 50	....	....	....	....
....	....	....	....	....	....	....
46 84	....	46 84	....	....	....	....
$210,796 73	....	$213,370 61	$9,298 71	67.22	31.41	1.37
....	....	$134 25	....	....	....	....
$54,468 57	....	54,468 57	....	....	....	....
10,149 89	....	10,149 89	....	....	....	....
783,605 11	....	783,605 11	....	....	....	....
17,610 48	....	17,610 48	....	....	....	....
208,252 28	....	208,252 28	....	....	....	....
166,940 78	....	166,940 78	....	....	....	....
360,055 29	....	360,055 29	....	....	....	....
....	....	....	....	....	....	....
4,673 99	$259,206 39	263,880 38	....	....	....	....
3,957 95	....	3,957 95	....	....	....	....
42,711 52	15,275 66	57,987 18	....	....	....	....
673 12	....	673 12	....	....	....	....
75,645 00	....	75,645 00	....	....	....	....
24,947 34	....	24,947 34	....	....	....	....
$1,753,691 32	$274,482 05	$2,028,307 62	$265,185 95	53.85	40.81	5.34
$804 82	....	$56,237 05	....	....	....	....
15,828 91	....	15,828 91	....	....	....	....
143,359 84	....	143,359 84	....	....	....	....
227,762 13	....	227,762 13	....	....	....	....
28,967 88	....	28,967 88	....	....	....	....

Class of Tax and Year of Action.	Amount of Levy.	Collections. Total.	Less Refunds and Over and Double Payments.	Net.	Discounts.
Personal Property—					
1905.........	....	20,599 61	....	20,599 61	....
1906.........	....	5,850 76	....	5,850 76	....
1907.........	....	1,527 39	....	1,527 39	....
1908.........	....	1,386 67	....	1,386 67	....
1909.........	....	1,065 99	....	1,065 99	....
1910.........	....	2,219 25	....	2,219 25	....
1911.........	....	116 05	....	116 05	....
1912.........	....	....	....	....	....
1913.........	....	....	....	....	....
1914.........	....	4,654 22	....	4,654 22	....
Totals...	$10,780,825 69	$7,624,473 00	$27,631 00	$7,596,842 00	$55,432 23

Part I-B—Recapitulation, Combining the Four Classes of Tax Shown in the Preced ing to Year of

Totals for—					
1900.........	$82,539,201 95	$60,082,493 74	$3,838 68	$60,078,655 06	$424,772 25
1901.........	....	8,818,604 59	58,740 79	8,759,863 80	....
1902.........	....	2,243,033 92	9,133 84	2,233,900 08	....
1903.........	....	1,006,173 15	3,193 10	1,002,980 05	....
1904.........	....	495,862 72	8,512 94	487,349 78	....
1905.........	....	2,410,913 80	15,003 84	2,395,909 96	....
1906.........	....	222,757 65	8,258 93	214,498 72	....
1907.........	....	323,035 65	7,129 55	315,906 10	....
1908.........	....	95,505 40	231 38	95,274 02	....
1909.........	....	190,058 71	17,587 45	172,471 26	....
1910.........	....	160,533 49	1,822 42	158,711 07	....
1911.........	....	126,403 87	24,764 35	101,639 52	....
1912.........	....	15,610 05	523 07	15,086 98	....
1913.........	....	12,654 08	1,530 21	11,123 87	....
1914.........	....	21,486 03	610 33	20,875 70	....
Grand Totals.	$82,539,201 95	$76,225,126 85	$160,880 88	$76,064,245 97	$424,772 25

TABLE III.—TAX

	Amount of Levy.	Collections. Total.	Less Refunds and Over and Double Payments.	Net.	Discounts.
			Part I.—Classified According to General		
Real Estate (Lands and Buildings)	$69,985,905 58	$69,299,414 97	$113,192 93	$69,186,222 04	$362,989 54
Real Estate of Corporations..	721,067 36	510,378 19	36,631 45	473,746 74	3,744 61
Special Franchise	4,925,291 84	2,655,136 07	119,754 57	2,535,381 50	61 34
Personal Property	12,609,537 08	7,232,954 99	205,953 36	7,027,001 63	42,499 93
Grand Totals........	$88,241,801 86	$79,697,884 22	$475,532 31	$79,222,351 91	$409,295 42
					Part II.—Classified
Manhattan	$62,699,302 27	$56,756,384 00	$236,941 60	$56,519,442 40	$313,275 88
The Bronx	3,610,912 43	3,373,421 12	15,140 72	3,358,280 40	13,433 99
Brooklyn	17,925,755 51	16,069,673 06	188,043 26	15,881,629 80	68,905 84
Queens	2,776,559 40	2,497,105 61	33,258 19	2,463,847 42	9,624 35
Richmond	1,229,272 25	1,001,300 43	2,148 54	999,151 89	4,055 36
Grand Totals........	$88,241,801 86	$79,697,884 22	$475,532 31	$79,222,351 91	$409,295 42

Cancellations.	Deductions Under Section 48, Tax Law.	Total.	Balance Uncollected at December 31, 1914.	Percentages. Net Collections to Levy.	Total Discounts, Cancellations and Deductions to Levy.	Uncollected Balance to Levy.
38,593 22	....	38,593 22	....	....	....	....
6,494 97	....	6,494 97	....	....	....	....
18,971 35	....	18,971 35	....	....	....	....
....	....	....	....	....	....	....
1,426 01	....	1,426 01	....	....	....	....
....	....	....	....	....	....	....
224 77	....	224 77	....	....	....	....
....	....	....	....	....	....	....
38 21	....	38 21	....	....	....	....
92 84	....	92 84	....	....	....	....
$482,564 95	....	$537,997 18	$2,645,986 51	70.47	4.99	24.54

ing Part (I-A), and Summarizing the Transactions of the Entire Levy of 1900 *Accord-*
Occurrence.

$4,096 13	....	$428,868 38	....	72.78	.52	....
94,011 32	....	94,011 32	....	10.61	.12	...
245,900 75	....	245,900 75	....	2.70	.30	...
1,101,759 09	....	1,101,759 09	....	1.22	1.34	....
62,250 73	....	62,250 73	....	.59	.08	....
266,566 87	....	266,566 87	....	2.90	.32	....
348,084 37	....	348,084 37	....	.26	.42	....
386,612 46	....	386,612 46	....	.38	.47	....
342 42	....	342 42	....	.12	.00	....
22,102 55	$259,206 39	281,308 94	....	.21	.34	....
10,179 91	....	10,179 91	....	.19	.02	....
44,743 94	15,275 66	60,019 60	....	.13	.07	....
6,408 48	....	6,408 48	....	.02	.00	....
78,175 72	....	78,175 72	....	.02	.09	....
61,848 66	....	61,848 66	....	.03	.07	....
$2,733,083 40	$274,482 05	$3,432,337 70	$3,042,618 28	92.16	4.16	3.68

LEVY OF 1901.

Cancellations.	Deductions Under Section 48, Tax Law.	Total.	Balance Uncollected at Dec. 31, 1914.	Percentages. Borough and Specific Levy to Total Levy.	Net Collections to Levy.	Total Discounts, Cancellations and Deductions to Levy.	Uncollected Balance to Levy.
Character of Taxable Property.							
$272,964 23	....	$635,953 77	$163,729 77	79.31	98.86	.91	.23
238,512 42	....	242,257 03	5,063 59	.82	65.70	33.60	.70
1,757,035 13	$550,908 44	2,308,004 91	81,905 43	5.58	51.48	46.86	1.66
1,134,876 47	....	1,177,376 40	4,405,159 05	14.29	55.74	9.33	34.93
$3,403,388 25	$550,908 44	$4,363,592 11	$4,655,857 84	100.00	89.78	4.94	5.28
According to Boroughs.							
$2,505,918 69	$361,127 88	$3,180,322 45	$2,999,537 42	71.05	90.14	5.07	4.79
53,410 20	9,533 59	76,377 78	176,254 25	4.09	93.00	2.12	4.88
712,752 53	180,246 97	961,905 34	1,082,220 37	20.31	88.59	5.37	6.04
92,543 21	....	102,167 56	210,544 42	3.15	88.74	3.68	7.58
38,763 62	....	42,818 98	187,301 38	1.40	81.28	3.48	15.24
$3,403,388 25	$550,908 44	$4,363,592 11	$4,655,857 84	100.00	89.78	4.94	5.28

Part III.—Classified According to Boroughs

	Amount of Levy.	Collections. Total.	Less Refunds and Over and Double Payments.	Net.	Discounts.
Manhattan.					
Real Estate (Lands and Buildings)	$48,950,701 30	$48,570,202 46	$80,023 76	$48,490,178 70	$274,809 40
Real Estate of Corporations..	274,162 78	86,891 76	6,488 52	80,403 24	366 91
Special Franchise	3,729,843 89	2,061,884 04	107,821 93	1,954,062 11	2 85
Personal Property	9,744,594 30	6,037,405 74	42,607 39	5,994,798 35	38,096 72
Totals	$62,699,302 27	$56,756,384 00	$236,941 60	$56,519,442 40	$313,275 88
The Bronx.					
Real Estate (Lands and Buildings)	$2,973,370 58	$2,950,032 68	$5,615 22	$2,944,417 46	$11,704 27
Real Estate of Corporations..	185,864 20	182,911 51	183 07	182,728 44	1,459 20
Special Franchise	173,018 29	130,042 89	9,342 43	120,700 46	35 35
Personal Property	278,659 36	110,434 04	....	110,434 04	235 17
Totals	$3,610,912 43	$3,373,421 12	$15,140 72	$3,358,280 40	$13,433 99
Brooklyn.					
Real Estate (Lands and Buildings)	$14,859,406 19	$14,657,177 00	$22,705 39	$14,634,471 61	$64,691 19
Real Estate of Corporations..	119,297 00	102,334 42	7,273 07	95,061 35	735 69
Special Franchise	837,996 91	373,215 67	2,073 55	371,142 12	12 91
Personal Property	2,109,055 41	936,945 97	155,991 25	780,954 72	3,466 05
Totals	$17,925,755 51	$16,069,673 06	$188,043 26	$15,881,629 80	$68,905 84
Queens.					
Real Estate (Lands and Buildings)	$2,286,644 53	$2,244,317 90	$2,733 00	$2,241,584 90	$8,437 20
Real Estate of Corporations..	103,267 97	101,050 41	22,686 79	78,363 62	855 88
Special Franchise	135,964 41	72,510 81	516 66	71,994 15	10 23
Personal Property	250,682 49	79,226 49	7,321 74	71,904 75	321 04
Totals	$2,776,559 40	$2,497,105 61	$33,258 19	$2,463,847 42	$9,624 35
Richmond.					
Real Estate (Lands and Buildings)	$915,782 98	$877,684 93	$2,115 56	$875,569 37	$3,347 48
Real Estate of Corporations..	38,475 41	37,190 09	....	37,190 09	326 93
Special Franchise	48,468 34	17,482 66	....	17,482 66	....
Personal Property	226,545 52	68,942 75	32 98	68,909 77	380 95
Totals	$1,229,272 25	$1,001,300 43	$2,148 54	$999,151 89	$4,055 36

Part I-A—Tax Levy of 1901—Supporting and Amplifying Totals Shown in Part I. Classified According to General Character of Taxable Property and Fur

Class of Tax and Year of Action.	Amount of Levy.	Collections. Total.	Less Refunds and Over and Double Payments.	Net.	Discounts.
Real Estate (Lands and Buildings)—					
1901	$69,985,905 58	$56,649,971 57	....	$56,649,971 57	$362,974 93
1902	....	8,561,221 59	$55,655 90	8,505,565 69	14 61
1903	....	1,941,686 78	10,541 80	1,931,144 98	....
1904	....	633,478 50	10,331 37	623,147 13	....
1905	....	705,190 24	6,439 03	698,751 21	....
1906	....	213,889 44	3,434 78	210,454 66	....
1907	....	311,695 96	2,184 40	309,511 56	....
1908	....	63,781 19	1,989 18	61,792 01	....
1909	....	90,899 41	16,453 08	74,446 33	....

Cancellations.	Deductions Under Section 48, Tax Law.	Total.	Balance Uncollected at Dec. 31, 1914.	Percentages. Borough and Specific Levy to Total Levy.	Net Collections to Levy.	Total Discounts, Cancellations and Deductions to Levy.	Uncollected Balance to Levy.
and General Character of Taxable Property.							
$95,502 07	....	$370,311 47	$90,211 13	55.47	99.06	.76	.18
193,246 68	....	193,613 59	145 95	.31	29.33	70.62	.05
1,413,042 99	$361,127 88	1,774,173 72	1,608 06	4.23	52.39	47.57	.04
804,126 95	....	842,223 67	2,907,572 28	11.04	61.52	8.64	29.84
$2,505,918 69	$361,127 88	$3,180,322 45	$2,999,537 42	71.05	90.14	5.07	4.79
$7,582 79	....	$19,287 06	$9,666 06	3.37	99.02	.65	.33
1,596 62	....	3,055 82	79 94	.22	98.31	1.65	.04
42,609 86	$9,533 59	52,178 80	139 03	.19	69.76	30.16	.08
1,620 93	....	1,856 10	166,369 22	.31	39.63	.66	59.71
$53,410 20	$9,533 59	$76,377 78	$176,254 25	4.09	93.00	2.12	4.88
$132,743 42	....	$197,434 61	$27,499 97	16.84	98.49	1.33	.18
18,845 47	....	19,581 16	4,654 49	.13	79.69	16.41	3.90
285,818 67	$180,246 97	466,078 55	776 24	.95	44.29	55.62	.09
275,344.97	....	278,811 02	1,049,289 67	2.39	37.03	13.22	49.75
$712,752 53	$180,246 97	$961,905 34	$1,082,220 37	20.31	88.59	5.37	6.04
$4,466 09	....	$12,903 29	$32,156 34	2.59	98.03	.56	1.41
23,865 26	....	24,721 14	183 21	.13	75.89	23.93	.18
11,321 94	....	11,332 17	52,638 09	.15	52.95	8.34	38.71
52,889 92	....	53,210 96	125,566 78	.28	28.69	21.22	50.09
$92,543 21	....	$102,167 56	$210,544 42	3.15	88.74	3.68	7.58
$32,669 86	....	$36,017 34	$4,196 27	1.04	95.61	3.93	.46
958 39	....	1,285 32	....	.04	96.66	3.34	......
4,241 67	....	4,241 67	26,744 01	.06	36.07	8.75	55.18
893 70	....	1,274 65	156,361 10	.26	30.42	.56	69.02
$38,763 62	....	$42,818 98	$187,301 38	1.40	81.28	3.48	15.24

of Table III., Showing All Transactions from October 7, 1901, *to December* 31, 1914, *ther Analyzed According to Year in Which Transactions Were Made.*

Cancellations.	Deductions Under Section 48, Tax Law.	Total.	Balance Uncollected at December 31, 1914.	Percentages. Net Collections to Levy.	Total Discounts, Cancellations and Deductions to Levy.	Un-Collected Balance to Levy.
$1,690 43	....	$364,665 36	....	....	....	....
119,690 51	....	119,705 12	....	....	....	....
58,874 93	....	58,874 93	....	....	....	....
22,180 98	....	22,180 98	....	....	....	....
11,815 60	....	11,815 60	....	....	....	....
9,927 62	....	9,927 62	....	....	....	....
2,702 17	....	2,702 17	....	....	....	....
7,693 46	....	7,693 46	....	....	....	....
18,094 13	....	18,094 13	....	....	....	....

Class of Tax and Year of Action.	Amount of Levy.	Collections.			Discounts.
		Total.	Less Refunds and Over and Double Payments.	Net.	
Real Estate (Lands and Buildings)—					
1910.........	....	59,657 66	2,082 29	57,575 37	....
1911.........	....	30,670 51	1,433 07	29,237 44	....
1912.........	....	17,798 65	617 49	17,181 16	....
1913.........	....	12,093 63	1,191 63	10,902 00	....
1914.........	....	7,379 84	838 91	6,540 93	....
Totals...	$69,985,905 58	$69,299,414 97	$113,192 93	$69,186,222 04	$362,989 54
Real Estate of Corporations—					
1901.........	$721,067 36	$423,013 02	$22,686 79	$400,326 23	$3,744 61
1002.........	....	13,525 04	....	13,525 04	....
1903.........	....	15,926 46	7,165 59	8,760 87	....
1904.........	....	27,912 41	183 07	27,729 34	....
1905.........	....	9,416 95	1,853 86	7,563 09	....
1906.........	....	15,511 12	4,634 66	10,876 46	....
1907.........	....	562 07	107 48	454 59	....
1908.........	....	1,272 79	....	1,272 79	....
1909.........	....	1,383 29	....	1,383 29	....
1910.........	....	933 41	....	933 41	....
1911.........	....	743 87	....	743 87	....
1912.........	....	47 77	....	47 77	....
1913.........	....	2 35	....	2 35	....
1914.........	....	127 64	....	127 64	....
Totals...	$721,067 36	$510,378 19	$36,631 45	$473,746 74	$3,744 61
Special Franchise—					
1901.........	$4,925,291 84	$99,299 52	....	$99,299 52	$61 34
1902.........	....	29,528 01	....	29,528 01	....
1903.........	....	3,109 33	....	3,109 33	....
1904.........	....	163,265 51	....	163,265 51	....
1905.........	....	1,540,348 70	$516 72	1,539,831 98	....
1906.........	....	44,737 91	....	44,737 91	....
1907.........	....	44,630 33	....	44,630 33	....
1908.........	....	37,222 17	....	37,222 17	....
1909.........	....	218,273 52	2,073 54	216,199 98	....
1910.........	....	350,182 26	117,164 31	233,017 95	....
1911.........	....	100,639 11	....	100,639 11	....
1912.........	....	2,458 99	....	2,458 99	....
1913.........	....	16,806 05	....	16,806 05	....
1914.........	....	4,634 66	....	4,634 66	....
Totals...	$4,925,291 84	$2,655,136 07	$119,754 57	$2,535,381 50	$61 34
Personal Property—					
1901.........	$12,609,537 08	$5,966,096 00	$36,624 43	$5,929,471 57	$42,499 93
1902.........	....	893,011 48	6,703 94	886,307 54	....
1903.........	....	282,354 50	162,116 68	120,237 82	....
1904.........	....	53,216 33	16 50	53,199 83	....
1905.........	....	26,050 46	358 28	25,692 18	....
1906.........	....	5,073 75	....	5,073 75	....
1907.........	....	1,564 90	133 53	1,431 37	....
1908.........	....	1,856 92	....	1,856 92	....
1909.........	....	643 46	....	643 46	....
1910.........	....	1,752 79	....	1,752 79	....

Cancellations.	Deductions Under Section 48, Tax Law.	Total.	Balance Uncollected at December 31, 1914.	Percentages. Net Collections to Levy.	Percentages. Total Discounts, Cancellations and Deductions to Levy.	Percentages. Un-Collected Balance to Levy.
2,567 74	....	2,567 74	....	....	....	....
831 13	....	831 13	....	....	....	....
1,798 45	....	1,798 45	....	....	....	....
2,586 62	....	2,586 62	....	....	....	....
12,510 46	....	12,510 46	....	....	....	....
$272,964 23	....	$635,953 77	$163,729 77	98.86	.91	.23
$611 49	....	$4,356 10	....	....	....	....
19,117 97	....	19,117 97	....	....	....	....
41,780 30	....	41,780 30	....	....	....	....
529 97	....	529 97	....	....	....	....
2,762 19	....	2,762 19	....	....	....	....
169,976 15	....	169,976 15	....	....	....	....
....	....	....	....	....	....	....
....	....	....	....	....	....	....
....	....	....	....	....	....	....
69 51	....	69 51	....	....	....	....
....	....	....	....	....	....	....
3,617 70	....	3,617 70	....	....	....	....
....	....	....	....	....	....	....
47 14	....	47 14	....	....	....	....
$238,512 42	....	$242,257 03	$5,063 59	65.70	33.60	.70
$49,094 66	....	$49,156 00	....	....	....	....
702 38	....	702 38	....	....	....	....
102,509 31	....	102,509 31	....	....	....	....
18,096 40	....	18,096 40	....	....	....	....
79,960 48	....	79,960 48	....	....	....	....
33,513 36	....	33,513 36	....	....	....	....
355,747 12	....	355,747 12	....	....	....	....
....	....	....	....	....	....	....
159,916 71	$511,967 91	671,884 62	....	....	....	....
341,025 41	24,254 62	365,280 03	....	....	....	....
537,082 35	14,685 91	551,768 26	....	....	....	....
806 12	....	806 12	....	....	....	....
76,858 84	....	76,858 84	....	....	....	....
1,721 99	....	1,721 99	....	....	....	....
$1,757,035 13	$550,908 44	$2,308,004 91	$81,905 43	51.48	46.86	1.66
$7,937 60	....	$50,437 53	....	....	....	....
76,614 78	....	76,614 78	....	....	....	....
346,661 93	....	346,661 93	....	....	....	....
270,200 02	....	270,200 02	....	....	....	....
132,983 72	....	132,983 72	....	....	....	....
15,376 51	....	15,376 51	....	....	....	....
281,862 66	....	281,862 66	....	....	....	....
....	....	....	....	....	....	....
....	....	....	....	....	....	....
1,158 66	....	1,158 66	....	....	....	....

Class of Tax and Year of Action.	Amount of Levy.	Collections. Total.	Collections. Less Refunds and Over and Double Payments.	Collections. Net.	Discounts.
Personal Property—					
1911.........	....	712 98	....	712 98	....
1912.........	....	602 57	....	602 57	....
1913.........	....	....	....	....	....
1914.........	....	18 85	....	18 85	....
Totals...	$12,609,537 08	$7,232,954 99	$205,953 36	$7,027,001 63	$42,499 93

Part I-B—Recapitulation—Combining the Four Classes of Tax Shown in the Preced According to Ye

Class of Tax and Year of Action.	Amount of Levy.	Total.	Less Refunds and Over and Double Payments.	Net.	Discounts.
Totals for—					
1901.........	$88,241,801 86	$63,138,380 11	$59,311 22	$63,079,068 89	$409,280 81
1902.........	....	9,497,286 12	62,359 84	9,434,926 28	14 61
1903.........	....	2,243,077 07	179,824 07	2,063,253 00	....
1904.........	....	877,872 75	10,530 94	867,341 81	....
1905.........	....	2,281,006 35	9,167 89	2,271,838 46	....
1906.........	....	279,212 22	8,069 44	271,142 78	....
1907.........	....	358,453 26	2,425 41	356,027 85	....
1908.........	....	104,133 07	1,989 18	102,143 89	....
1909.........	....	311,199 68	18,526 62	292,673 06	....
1910.........	....	412,526 12	119,246 60	293,279 52	....
1911.........	....	132,766 47	1,433 07	131,333 40	....
1912.........	....	20,907 98	617 49	20,290 49	....
1913.........	....	28,902 03	1,191 63	27,710 40	....
1914.........	....	12,160 99	838 91	11,322 08	....
Grand Totals	$88,241,801 86	$79,697,884 22	$475,532 31	$79,222,351 91	$409,295 42

TABLE IV.—TAX

	Amount of Levy.	Collections. Total.	Collections. Less Refunds and Over and Double Payments.	Collections. Net.	Discounts.
			Part I.—Classified According to General		
Real Estate (Lands and Buildings)	$70,550,043 48	$69,992,970 15	$107,062 79	$69,885,907 36	$384,761 17
Real Estate of Corporations..	704,173 61	502,652 17	48,483 60	454,168 57	3,983 96
Special Franchise	5,049,106 47	2,593,710 59	6,506 59	2,587,204 00	130 23
Personal Property	11,925,231 36	6,341,709 18	9,699 08	6,332,010 10	40,053 18
Grand Totals........	$88,228,554 92	$79,431,042 09	$171,752 06	$79,259,290 03	$428,928 54
				Part II.—Classified	
Manhattan	$62,905,554 41	$56,704,084 04	$98,040 02	$56,606,044 02	$327,592 79
The Bronx	3,775,718 17	3,432,680 30	8,927 63	3,423,752 67	14,922 20
Brooklyn	17,753,465 53	15,864,304 62	38,515 20	15,825,789 42	72,344 42
Queens	2,730,101 63	2,501,633 39	24,863 17	2,476,770 22	10,158 88
Richmond	1,063,715 18	928,339 74	1,406 04	926,933 70	3,910 25
Grand Totals........	$88,228,554 92	$79,431,042 09	$171,752 06	$79,259,290 03	$428,928 54
Manhattan.			*Part III.—Classified According to Boroughs*		
Real Estate (Lands and Buildings)	$49,556,162 93	$49,153,819 96	$80,415 99	$49,073,403 97	$291,622 26
Real Estate of Corporations..	271,925 78	81,725 45	8,070 71	73,654 74	398 88
Special Franchise	3,800,492 03	1,972,022 12	400 39	1,971,621 73	6 78
Personal Property	9,276,973 67	5,496,516 51	9,152 93	5,487,363 58	35,564 87
Totals	$62,905,554 41	$56,704,084 04	$98,040 02	$56,606,044 02	$327,592 79

Cancellations.	Deductions Under Section 48, Tax Law.	Total.	Balance Uncollected at December 31, 1914.	Percentages. Net Collections to Levy.	Total Discounts, Cancellations and Deductions to Levy.	Un-Collected Balance to Levy.
463 46	....	463 46	....	....	....	....
188 14	....	188 14	....	....	....	....
309 56	....	309 56	....	....	....	....
1,119 43	....	1,119 43	....	....	....	....
$1,134,876 47	....	$1,177,376 40	$4,405,159 05	55.74	9.33	34 93

ing Part (I-A) and Summarizing the Transactions of the Entire Levy of 1901 *ar of Occurrence.*

Cancellations.	Deductions Under Section 48, Tax Law.	Total.	Balance Uncollected at December 31, 1914.	Net Collections to Levy.	Total Discounts, Cancellations and Deductions to Levy.	Un-Collected Balance to Levy.
$59,334 18	....	$468,614 99	....	....	....	....
216,125 64	....	216,140 25	....	....	....	....
549,826 47	....	549,826 47	....	....	....	....
311,007 37	....	311,007 37	....	....	....	....
227,521 99	....	227,521 99	....	....	....	....
228,793 64	....	228,793 64	....	....	....	....
640,311 95	....	640,311 95	....	....	....	....
7,693 46	....	7,693 46	....	....	....	....
178,010 84	$511,967 91	689,978 75	....	....	....	....
344,821 32	24,254 62	369,075 94	....	....	....	....
538,376 94	14,685 91	553,062 85	....	....	....	....
6,410 41	....	6,410 41	....	....	....	....
79,755 02	....	79,755 02	....	....	....	....
15,399 02	....	15,399 02	....	....	....	....
$3,403,388 25	$550,908 44	$4,363,592 11	$4,655,857 84	89.78	4.94	5.28

Levy of 1902.

Cancellations.	Deductions Under Section 48, Tax Law.	Total.	Balance Uncollected at Dec. 31, 1914.	Percentages. Borough and Specific Levy to Total Levy.	Net Collections to Levy.	Total Discounts, Cancellations and Deductions to Levy.	Un-collected Balance to Levy.
Character of Taxable Property.							
$149,831 39	....	$534,592 56	$129,543 56	79.97	99.06	.76	.18
241,143 78	....	245,127 74	4,877 30	.79	64.50	34.81	.69
1,837,558 76	$565,382 21	$2,403,071 20	58,831 27	5.72	51.24	47.60	1.16
1,315,269 77	....	1,355,322 95	4,237,898 31	13.52	53.09	11.37	35.54
$3,543,803 70	$565,382 21	$4,538,114 45	$4,431,150 44	100.00	89.84	5.14	5.02
According to Boroughs.							
$2,629,228 72	$375,354 54	$3,332,176 05	$2,967,334 34	71.29	89.99	5.29	4.72
115,878 94	11,887 19	142,688 33	209,277 17	4.28	90.68	3.78	5.54
715,644 49	178,140 48	966,129 39	961,546 72	20.13	89.14	5.44	5.42
74,056 79	....	84,215 67	169,115 74	3.09	90.72	3.08	6.20
8,994 76	....	12,905 01	123,876 47	1.21	87.14	1.21	11.65
$3,543,803 70	$565,382 21	$4,538,114 45	$4,431,150 44	100.00	89.84	5.14	5.02
and General Character of Taxable Property.							
$130,568 99	....	$422,191 25	$60,567 71	56.17	99.03	.85	.12
197,751 70	....	198,150 58	120 46	.31	27.09	72.87	.04
1,450,832 51	$375,354 54	1,826,193 83	2,676 47	4.31	51.88	48.05	.07
850,075 52	....	885,640 39	2,903,969 70	10.50	59.15	9.55	31.30
$2,629,228 72	$375,354 54	$3,332,176 05	$2,967,334 34	71.29	89.99	5.29	4.72

	Amount of Levy.	Collections. Total.	Collections. Less Refunds and Over and Double Payments.	Collections. Net.	Discounts.
The Bronx.					
Real Estate (Lands and Buildings)	$3,100,805 05	$3,074,652 20	$8,520 69	$3,066,131 51	$13,213 00
Real Estate of Corporations..	182,475 85	179,513 01	179 60	179,333 41	1,484 02
Special Franchise	206,239 53	126,734 58	....	126,734 58	30 13
Personal Property	286,197 74	51,780 51	227 34	51,553 17	195 05
Totals	$3,775,718 17	$3,432,680 30	$8,927 63	$3,423,752 67	$14,922 20
Brooklyn.					
Real Estate (Lands and Buildings)	$14,761,825 36	$14,683,592 79	$14,251 66	$14,669,341 13	$67,715 89
Real Estate of Corporations..	109,905 26	103,602 84	17,915 05	85,687 79	889 99
Special Franchise	883,102 84	403,075 45	6,029 68	397,045 77	68 82
Personal Property	1,998,632 07	674,033 54	318 81	673,714 73	3,669 72
Totals	$17,753,465 53	$15,864,304 62	$38,515 20	$15,825,789 42	$72,344 42
Queens.					
Real Estate (Lands and Buildings)	$2,301,085 49	$2,260,365 02	$2,468 41	$2,257,896 61	$8,913 36
Real Estate of Corporations..	100,439 03	99,063 14	22,318 24	76,744 90	875 74
Special Franchise	122,078 65	74,057 15	76 52	73,980 63	17 57
Personal Property	206,498 46	68,148 08	....	68,148 08	352 21
Totals	$2,730,101 63	$2,501,633 39	$24,863 17	$2,476,770 22	$10,158 88
Richmond.					
Real Estate (Lands and Buildings)	$830,164 65	$820,540 18	$1,406 04	$819,134 14	$3,296 66
Real Estate of Corporations..	39,427 69	38,747 73	....	38,747 73	335 33
Special Franchises	37,193 42	17,821 29	....	17,821 29	6 93
Personal Property	156,929 42	51,230 54	....	51,230 54	271 33
Total	$1,063,715 18	$928,339 74	$1,406 04	$926,933 70	$3,910 25

Part I-A—Tax Levy of 1902, Supporting and Amplifying Totals Shown in Part I Classified According to General Character of Taxable Property and

Class of Tax and Year of Action.	Amount of Levy.	Collections. Total.	Collections. Less Refunds and Over and Double Payments.	Collections. Net.	Discounts.
Real Estate (Lands and Buildings)—					
1902.........	$70,550,043 48	$58,066,471 53	....	$58,066,471 53	$384,761 17
1903.........	....	8,216,431 13	$55,837 52	8,160,593 61	....
1904.........	....	1,825,210 38	8,285 74	1,816,924 64	....
1905.........	....	887,547 78	15,122 41	872,425 37	....
1906.........	....	356,959 63	8,050 76	348,908 87	....
1909.........	....	175,606 81	3,959 30	171,647 51	....
1908.........	....	110,004 09	1,801 15	108,202 94	....
1909.........	....	173,087 45	6,849 23	166,238 22	....
1910.........	....	82,379 97	1,428 41	80,951 56	....
1911.........	....	46,877 77	1,705 43	45,172 34	....
1912.........	....	23,690 93	704 19	22,986 74	....
1913.........	....	17,722 74	1,201 63	16,521 11	....
1914.........	....	10,979 94	2,117 02	8,862 92	....
Totals...	$70,550,043 48	$69,992,970 15	$107,062 79	$69,885,907 36	$384,761 17

Cancellations.	Deductions Under Section 48, Tax Law.	Total.	Balance Uncollected at Dec. 31, 1914.	Percentages. Borough and Specific Levy to Total Levy.	Net Collections to Levy.	Total Discounts, Cancellations and Deductions to Levy.	Uncollected Balance to Levy.
$6,085 32	....	$19,298 32	$15,375 22	3.52	98.88	.62	.50
1,566 37	....	3,050 39	92 05	.21	98.28	1.67	.05
66,579 38	$11,887 19	78,496 70	1,008 25	.23	61.45	38.06	.49
41,647 87	....	41,842 92	192,801 65	.32	18.01	14.62	67.37
$115,878 94	$11,887 19	$142,688 33	$209,277 17	4.28	90.68	3.78	5.54
$9,466 80	....	$77,182 69	$15,301 54	16.73	99.37	.53	.10
18,879 98	....	19,769 97	4,447 50	.13	77.97	17.99	4.04
304,786 82	$178,140 48	482,996 12	3,060 95	1.00	44.97	54.69	.34
382,510 89	....	386,180 61	938,736 73	2.27	33.71	19.32	46.97
$715,644 49	$178,140 48	$966,129 39	$961,546 72	20.13	89.14	5.44	5.42
$2,477 12	....	$11,390 51	$31,798 37	2.61	98.12	.50	1.38
22,601 10	....	23,476 84	217 29	.11	76.41	23.37	.22
12,701 03	....	12,718 60	35,379 42	.14	60.60	10.42	28.98
36,277 51	....	36,629 72	101,720 66	.23	33.00	17.74	49.26
$74,056 79	....	$84,215 67	$169,115 74	3.09	90.72	3.08	6.20
$1,233 13	....	$4,529 79	$6,500 72	.95	98.67	.55	.78
344 63	....	679 96	....	.04	98.27	1.73	......
2,659 02	....	2,665 95	16,706 18	.04	47.92	7.16	44.92
4,757 08	....	5,029 31	100,669 57	.18	32.64	3.21	64.15
$8,994 76	....	$12,905 01	$123,876 47	1.21	87.14	1.21	11.65

of Table IV, Showing All Transactions from October 6, 1902, *to December* 31, 1914, *Further Analyzed According to Year in Which Transactions Were Made.*

Cancellations.	Deductions Under Section 48, Tax Law.	Total.	Balance Uncollected at December 31, 1914.	Percentages. Net Collections to Levy.	Total Discounts, Cancellations and Deductions to Levy.	Un-Collected Balance to Levy.
$7,217 26	....	$391,978 43	....	....	....	....
29,720 66	....	29,720 66	....	....	....	....
21,841 67	....	21,841 67	....	....	....	....
21,258 77	....	21,258 77	....	....	....	....
16,288 85	....	16,288 85	....	....	....	....
4,277 33	....	4,277 33	....	....	....	....
2,065 99	....	2,065 99	....	....	....	....
12,288 77	....	12,288 77	....	....	....	....
2,454 06	....	2,454 06	....	....	....	....
1,510 40	....	1,510 40	....	....	....	....
3,152 22	....	3,152 22	....	....	....	....
2,906 62	....	2,906 62	....	....	....	....
24,848 79	....	24,848 79	....	....	....	....
$149,831 39	....	$534,592 56	$129,543 56	99.06	.76	.18

Class of Tax and Year of Action.	Amount of Levy.	Collections. Total.	Collections. Less Refunds and Over and Double Payments.	Collections. Net.	Discounts.
Real Estate of Corporations—					
1902.........	$704,173 61	$446,045 37	$38,557 59	$407,487 78	$3,983 96
1903.........	....	245 93	....	245 93	....
1904.........	....	28,350 54	3,703 43	24,647 11	....
1905.........	....	4,511 41	....	4,511 41	....
1906.........	....	15,451 77	6,116 68	9,335 09	....
1907.........	....	1,627 74	105 90	1,521 84	....
1908.........	....	1,260 87	....	1,260 87	....
1909.........	....	1,539 35	....	1,539 35	....
1910.........	....	1,338 36	....	1,338 36	....
1911.........	....	749 12	....	749 12	....
1912.........	....	1,401 91	....	1,401 91	....
1913.........	....	4 54	....	4 54	....
1914.........	....	125 26	....	125 26	....
Totals...	$704,173 61	$502,652 17	$48,483 60	$454,168 57	$3,983 96
Special Franchise—					
1902.........	$5,049,106 47	$123,550 27	....	$123,550 27	$130 23
1903.........	....	5,257 60	....	5,257 60	....
1904.........	....	16,088 99	....	16,088 99	....
1905.........	....	1,120,593 09	6,106 18	1,114,486 91	....
1906.........	....	76,546 60	....	76,546 60	....
1907.........	....	157,762 05	....	157,762 05	....
1908.........	....	74,950 40	....	74,950 40	....
1909.........	....	211,225 59	....	211,225 59	....
1910.........	....	455,634 99	400 41	455,234 58	....
1911.........	....	323,041 80	....	323,041 80	....
1912.........	....	811 11	....	881 11	....
1913.........	....	23,062 86	....	23,062 86	....
1914.........	....	5,115 24	....	5,115 24	....
Totals...	$5,049,106 47	$2,593,710 59	$6,506 59	$2,587,204 00	$130 23
Personal Property—					
1902.........	$11,925,231 36	$5,609,470 02	$7,560 07	$5,601,909 95	$40,053 18
1903.........	....	581,125 37	483 11	580,642 26	....
1904.........	....	89,670 94	752 44	88,918 50	....
1905.........	....	48,851 16	227 34	48,623 82	....
1906.........	....	6,317 31	....	6,317 31	....
1907.........	....	1,155 68	....	1,155 68	....
1908.........	....	1,873 22	....	1,873 22	....
1909.........	....	140 40	....	140 40	....
1910.........	....	1,292 56	676 12	616 44	....
1911.........	....	454 68	....	454 68	....
1912.........	....	1,013 92	....	1,013 92	....
1913.........	....	226 25	....	226 25	....
1914.........	....	117 67	....	117 67	....
Totals...	$11,925,231 36	$6,341,709 18	$9.699 08	$6,332.010 10	$40.053 18

Part I-B—Recapitulation—Combining the Four Classes of Tax Shown in the Preceding
to Year of

Totals for—					
1902.........	$88,228,554 92	$64,245,537 19	$46,117 66	$64,199,419 53	$428,928 54
1903.........	....	8,803,060 03	56,320 63	8,746,739 40	....

Cancellations.	Deductions Under Section 48, Tax Law.	Total.	Balance Uncollected at December 31, 1914.	Percentages. Net Collections to Levy.	Percentages. Total Discounts, Cancellations and Deductions to Levy.	Percentages. Un-Collected Balance to Levy.
....	....	$3,983 96	....	....	....	....
$38,557 59	....	38,557 59	....	....	....	....
179 60	....	179 60	....	....	....	....
23,291 94	....	23,291 94	....	....	....	....
166,779 55	....	166,779 55	....	....	....	....
....	....	....	....	....	....	....
....	....	....	....	....	....	....
344 63	....	344 63	....	....	....	....
1,637 99	....	1,637 99	....	....	....	....
....	....	....	....	....	....	....
8,487 36	....	8,487 36	....	....	....	....
....	....	....	....	....	....	....
1,865 12	....	1,865 12	....	....	....	....
$241,143 78	....	$245,127 74	$4,877 30	64.50	34.81	.69
$58,394 80	....	$58,525 03	....	....	....	....
105,670 75	....	105,670 75	....	....	....	....
19,169 03	....	19,169 03	....	....	....	....
78,082 58	....	78,082 58	....	....	....	....
40,153 82	....	40,153 82	....	....	....	....
349,674 72	....	349,674 72	....	....	....	....
....	11,887 19	11,887 19	....	....	....	....
173,725 08	541,346 20	715,071 28	....	....	....	....
377,166 55	....	377,166 55	....	....	....	....
557,525 42	12,148 82	569,674 24	....	....	....	....
888 45	....	888 45	....	....	....	....
75,398 64	....	75,398 64	....	....	....	....
1,708 92	....	1,708 92	....	....	....	....
$1,837,558 76	$565,382 21	$2,403,071 20	$58,831 27	51.24	47.60	1.16
$16,605 88	....	$56,659 06	....	....	....	....
158,773 44	....	158,773 44	....	....	....	....
588,734 92	....	588,734 92	....	....	....	....
190,556 95	....	190,556 95	....	....	....	....
16,465 47	....	16,465 47	....	....	....	....
339,080 52	....	339,080 52	....	....	....	....
2,256 13	....	2,256 13	....	....	....	....
....	....	....	....	....	....	....
....	....	....	....	....	....	....
454 68	....	454 68	....	....	....	....
62 27	....	62 27	....	....	....	....
572 35	....	572 35	....	....	....	....
1,707 16	....	1,707 16	....	....	....	....
$1,315,269 77	....	$1,355,322 95	$4,237,898 31	53.09	11.37	35.54

Part (I-A), and Summarizing the Transactions of the Entire Levy of 1902, *According Occurrence.*

Cancellations.	Deductions Under Section 48, Tax Law.	Total.	Balance Uncollected at December 31, 1914.	Net Collections to Levy.	Total Discounts, Cancellations and Deductions to Levy.	Un-Collected Balance to Levy.
$82,217 94	....	$511,146 48	....	72.76	.58	....
332,722 44	....	332,722 44	....	9.91	.38	....

Class of Tax and Year of Action.	Amount of Levy.	Collections. Total.	Collections. Less Refunds and Over and Double Payments.	Collections. Net.	Discounts.
Totals for—					
1904.........	....	1,959,320 85	12,741 61	1,946,579 24	....
1905.........	....	2,061,503 44	21,455 93	2,040,047 51	....
1906.........	....	455,275 31	14,167 44	441,107 87	....
1907.........	....	336,152 28	4,065 20	332,087 08	....
1908.........	....	188,088 58	1,801 15	186,287 43	....
1909.........	....	385,992 79	6,849 23	379,143 56	....
1910.........	....	540,645 88	2,504 94	538,140 94	....
1911.........	....	371,123 37	1,705 43	369,417 94	....
1912.........	....	26,987 87	704 19	26,283 68	....
1913.........	....	41,016 39	1,201 63	39,814 76	....
1914.........	....	16,338 11	2,117 02	14,221 09	....
Grand Totals.	$88,228,554 92	$79,431,042 09	$171,752 06	$79,259,290 03	$428,928 54

TABLE V.—TAX

	Amount of Levy.	Collections. Total.	Collections. Less Refunds and Over and Double Payments.	Collections. Net.	Discounts.
			Part I.—Classified According		*to General*
Real Estate (Lands and Buildings)	$64,149,021 06	$63,441,561 69	$103,664 75	$63,337,896 94	$361.579 03
Real Estate of Corporations..	418,359 13	393,671 01	7,283 03	386,387 98	3,335 74
Special Franchise	3,360,543 42	2,275,012 46	18,243 34	2,256,769 12	1,091 56
Personal Property	9,703,850 94	4,956,024 42	1,270 45	4,954,753 97	32,553 28
Grand Totals	$77,631,774 55	$71,066,269 58	$130,461 57	$70,935,808 01	$398,559 61
					Part II.—Classified
Manhattan	$57,014,987 49	$52,218,819 35	$77,442 73	$52,141,376 62	$310,019 34
Bronx	3,701,364 75	3,471,846 52	9,893 52	3,461,953 00	15,910 48
Brooklyn	14,204,464 98	12,899,368 46	39,369 90	12,859,998 56	61.460 38
Queens	1,975,354 56	1,813,934 53	3,203 46	1,810,731 07	8,041 24
Richmond	735,602 77	662,300 72	551 96	661,748 76	3,128 17
Grand Totals	$77,631,774 55	$71,066,269 58	$130,461 57	$70,935,808 01	$398,559 61
Manhattan.		*Part III.—Classified*	*According*	*to*	*Boroughs*
Real Estate (Lands and Buildings)	$46,674,494 04	$46,145,779 85	$71,366 60	$46,074,413 25	$280,022 23
Real Estate of Corporations..	65,881 49	52,768 17	3,534 17	49,234 00	355 04
Special Franchise	2,508,524 34	1,736,667 03	1,375 67	1,735,291 36	829 44
Personal Property	7,766,087 62	4,283,604 30	1,166 29	4,282,438 01	28,812 63
Total	$57,014,987 49	$52,218,819 35	$77,442 73	$52,141,376 62	$310,019 34
The Bronx.					
Real Estate (Lands and Buildings)	$3,188,779 26	$3,153,765 11	$6,162 88	$3,147,602 23	$14,191 59
Real Estate of Corporations..	168,700 54	166,259 31	3,660 99	162,598 32	1,423 73
Special Franchise	135,331 92	106,223 96	69 65	106,154 31	79 94
Personal Property	208,553 03	45,598 14	....	45,598 14	215 22
Total	$3,701,364 75	$3,471,846 52	$9,893 52	$3,461,953 00	$15,910 48
Brooklyn.					
Real Estate (Lands and Buildings)	$12,012,167 60	$11,910,496 93	$23,132 17	$11,887,364 76	$57,539 20
Real Estate of Corporations..	90,622 92	83,591 69	87 87	83,503 82	750 85
Special Franchise	612,531 62	364,449 40	16,149 57	348.299 83	131 81
Personal Property	1,489,142 84	540.830 44	29	540,830 15	3,038 52
Total	$14,204,464 98	$12,899,368 46	$39,369 90	$12,859,998 56	$61,460 38

Cancellations.	Deductions Under Section 48, Tax Law.	Total.	Balance Uncollected at December 31, 1914.	Percentages. Net Collections to Levy.	Total Discounts, Cancellations and Deductions to Levy.	Un-Collected Balance to Levy.
629,925 22	....	629,925 22	....	2.26	.71	....
313,190 24	....	313,190 24	....	2.31	.36	....
239,687 69	....	239,687 69	....	.49	.27	....
693,032 57	....	693,032 57	....	.37	.78	....
4,322 12	11,887 19	16,209 31	....	.21	.02	....
186,358 48	541,346 20	727,704 68	....	.43	.82	....
381,258 60	....	381,258 60	....	.61	.43	....
559,490 50	12,148 82	571,639 32	....	.41	.64	....
12,590 30	....	12,590 30	....	.03	.02	....
78,877 61	....	78,877 61	....	.04	.09	....
30,129 99	....	30,129 99	....	.01	.04	....
$3,543,803 70	$565,382 21	$4,538,114 45	$4,431,150 44	89.84	5.14	5.02

Levy of 1903.

Cancellations.	Deductions Under Section 48, Tax Law.	Total.	Balance Uncollected at Dec. 31, 1914.	Percentages. Borough and Specific Levy to Total Levy.	Net Collections to Levy.	Total Discounts, Cancellations and Deductions to Levy.	Un-collected Balance to Levy.
Character of Taxable Property.							
$289,160 65	....	$650,739 68	$160,384 44	82.63	98.73	1.02	.25
20,436 16	....	23,771 90	8,199 25	.54	92.37	5.68	1.95
524,541 02	$539,940 30	1,065,572 88	38,201 42	4.33	67.16	31.71	1.13
859,323 75	....	891,877 03	3,857,219 94	12.50	51.06	9.19	39.75
$1,693,461 58	$539,940 30	$2,631,961 49	$4,064,005 05	100.00	91.37	.39	5.24
According to Boroughs.							
1,328,192 67	$358,673 66	$1,996,885 67	$2,876,725 20	73.45	91.45	3.50	5.05
48,608 34	13,040 52	77,559 34	161,852 41	4.77	93.54	2.09	4.37
261,616 34	168,226 12	491,302 84	853,163 58	18.29	90.54	3.46	6.00
50,457 66	....	58,498 90	106,124 59	2.54	91.67	2.96	5.37
4,586 57	....	7,714 74	66,139 27	.95	89.96	1.05	8.99
$1,693,461 58	$539,940 30	$2,631,961 49	$4,064,005 05	100.00	91.37	3.39	5.24
and General Character of Taxable Property.							
$235,208 65	....	$515,230 88	$84,849 91	60.12	98.72	1.10	.18
13,337 93	....	13,692 97	2,954 52	.09	74.73	20.79	4.48
412,366 82	$358,673 66	771,869 92	1,363 06	3.23	69.17	30.77	.06
667,279 27	....	696,091 90	2,787,557 71	10.01	55.15	8.96	35.89
$1,328,192 67	$358,673 66	$1,996,885 67	$2,876,725 20	73.45	91.45	3.50	5.05
$10,163 63	....	$24,355 22	$16,821 81	4.11	98.71	.76	.53
4,536 44	....	5,960 17	142 05	.22	96.38	3.53	.09
11,597 74	$13,040 52	24,718 20	4,459 41	.17	78.44	18.26	3.30
22,310 53	....	22,525 75	140,429 14	.27	21.86	10.81	67.33
$48,608 34	$13,040 52	$77,559 34	$161,852 41	4.79	93.54	2.09	4.37
$35,434 04	....	$92,973 24	$31,829 60	15.46	98.96	.77	.27
1,541 55	....	2,292 40	4,826 70	.12	92.14	2.53	5.33
94,494 08	$168,226 12	262,852 01	1,379 78	.79	56.86	42.91	.23
130,146 67	....	133,185 19	815,127 50	1.92	36.32	8.94	54.74
$261,616 34	$168,226 12	$491,302 84	$853,163 58	18.29	90.54	3.46	6.00

	Amount of Levy.	Collections. Total.	Collections. Less Refunds and Over and Double Payments.	Collections. Net.	Discounts.
Queens.					
Real Estate (Lands and Buildings)	$1,677,292 33	$1,643,794 09	$2,466 10	$1,641,327 99	$7,155 86
Real Estate of Corporations..	66,710 43	65,057 33	....	65,057 33	582 88
Special Franchise	81,542 32	54,854 54	648 45	54,206 09	32 10
Personal Property	149,809 48	50,228 57	88 91	50,139 66	270 40
Total	$1,975,354 56	$1,813,934 53	$3,203 46	$1,810,731 07	$8,041 24
Richmond.					
Real Estate (Lands and Buildings)	$596,287 83	$587,725 71	$537 00	$587,188 71	$2,670 15
Real Estate of Corporations..	26,443 75	25,994 51	....	25,994 51	223 24
Special Franchise	22,613 22	12,817 53	....	12,817 53	18 27
Personal Property	90,257 97	35,762 97	14 96	35,748 01	216 51
Total	$735,602 77	$662,300 72	$551 96	$661,748 76	$3,128 17

Part I-A—Tax Levy of 1903, *Supporting and Amplifying Totals Shown in Part I. Classified According to General Character of Taxable Property and*

Class of Tax and Year of Action.	Amount of Levy.	Collections. Total.	Collections. Less Refunds and Over and Double Payments.	Collections. Net.	Discounts.
Real Estate (Land and Buildings)—					
1903.........	$64,149,021 06	$53,306,442 96	....	$53,306,442 96	$361,537 66
1904.........	....	7,064,202 56	$52,130 04	7,012,072 52	41 37
1905.........	....	1,557,721 87	10,581 26	1,547,140 61	....
1906.........	....	567,937 20	4,970 46	562,966 74	....
1907.........	....	295,369 67	1,743 17	293,626 50	....
1908.........	....	202,757 00	9,305 62	193,451 38	....
1909.........	....	249,300 78	7,548 59	241,752 19	....
1910.........	....	100,675 22	12,152 63	88,522 59	....
1911.........	....	49,126 22	1,435 37	47,690 85	....
1912.........	....	22,242 52	640 00	21,602 52	....
1913.........	....	16,812 10	1,472 94	15,339 16	....
1914.........	....	8,973 59	1,684 67	7,288 92	....
Totals...	$64,149,021 06	$63,441,561 69	$103,664 75	$63,337,896 94	$361,579 03
Real Estate of Corporations—					
1903.........	$418,359 13	$359,225 16	$13 40	$359,211 76	$3,335 74
1904.........	....	24,539 22	7,194 16	17,345 06	....
1905.........	....	1,892 89	....	1,892 89	....
1906.........	....	3,192 82	....	3,192 82	....
1907.........	....	357 96	74 47	283 49	....
1908.........	....	821 28	....	821 28	....
1909.........	....	1,051 91	....	1,051 91	....
1910.........	....	888 26	....	888 26	....
1911.........	....	494 02	1 00	493 02	....
1912.........	....	1,183 17	....	1,183 17	....
1913.........	....	16 95	....	16 95	....
1914.........	....	7 37	....	7 37	....
Totals...	$418,359 13	$393,671 01	$7,283 03	$386.387 98	$3,335 74

Cancellations.	Deductions Under Section 48, Tax Law.	Total.	Balance Uncollected at Dec. 31, 1914.	Percentages. Borough and Specific Levy to Total Levy.	Net Collections to Levy.	Total Discounts, Cancellations and Deductions to Levy.	Uncollected Balance to Levy.
$5,941 41	....	$13,097 27	$22,867 07	2.16	97.86	.78	1.36
799 47	....	1,382 35	270 75	.08	97.52	2.07	.41
5,060 94	....	5,093 04	22,243 19	.11	66.48	6.24	27.28
38,655 84	....	38,926 24	60,743 58	.19	33.47	25.98	40 55
$50,457 66	....	$58,498 90	$106,124 59	2.54	91.67	2.96	5.37
$2,412 92	....	$5,083 07	$4,016 05	.76	98.48	.85	.67
220 77	....	444 01	5 23	.04	98.30	1.68	.02
1,021 44	....	1,039 71	8,755 98	.03	56.69	4.59	38.72
931 44	....	1,147 95	53,362 01	.12	39.61	1.27	59.12
$4,586 57	....	$7,714 74	$66,139 27	.95	89.96	1.05	8.99

of Table V., Showing All Transactions from October 5, 1903, *to December* 31, 1914, *Further Analyzed According to Year in Which Transactions Were Made.*

Cancellations.	Deductions Under Section 48, Tax Law	Total.	Balance Uncollected at December 31, 1914.	Percentages. Net Collections to Levy.	Total Discounts. Cancellations and Deductions to Levy.	Un-Collected Balance to Levy.
$19,353 71	....	$380,891 37	....	....	....	....
63,890 59	....	63,931 96	....	....	....	....
31,666 97	....	31,666 97	....	....	....	....
29,859 79	....	29,859 79	....	....	....	....
33,529 73	....	33,529 73	....	....	....	....
9,812 07	....	9,812 07	....	....	....	....
21,068 17	....	21,068 17	....	....	....	....
6,278 92	....	6,278 92	....	....	....	....
8,543 74	....	8,543 74	....	....	....	....
14,410 07	....	14,410 07	....	....	....	....
18,306 39	....	18,306 39	....	....	....	....
32,440 50	....	32,440 50	....	....	....	....
$289,160 65	....	$650,739 68	$160,384 44	98.73	1.02	.25
....	....	$3,335 74	....	....	....	....
$125 82	....	125 82	....	....	....	....
2,710 95	....	2,710 95	....	....	....	....
2,191 18	....	2,191 18	....	....	....	....
863 87	....	863 87	....	....	....	....
....	....	....	....	....	....	....
7,289 11	....	7,289 11	....	....	....	....
42 40	....	42 40	....	....	....	....
....	....	....	....	....	....	....
4,249 68	....	4,249 68	....	....	....	....
....	....	....	....	....	....	....
2,963 15	....	2,963 15	....	....	....	....
$20,436 16	....	$23,771 90	$8,199 25	92.37	5.68	1.95

Class of Tax and Year of Action.	Amount of Levy.	Collections. Total.	Collections. Less Refunds and Over and Double Payments.	Collections. Net.	Discounts.
Special Franchises—					
1903.........	$3,360,543 42	$120,552 38	$22 34	$120,530 04	$1,091 56
1904.........	....	8,812 66	....	8,812 66	....
1905.........	....	381,646 58	648 45	380,998 13	....
1906.........	....	43,043 29	15,385 86	27,657 43	....
1907.........	....	596,242 76	....	596,242 76	....
1908.........	....	15,452 58	....	15,452 58	....
1909.........	....	135,016 55	....	135,016 55	....
1910.........	....	588,502 17	2,186 69	586,315 48	....
1911.........	....	355,992 09	....	355,992 09	....
1912.........	....	942 22	....	942 22	....
1913.........	....	28,809 18	....	28,809 18	....
1914.........	....	....	....	....	....
Total.	$3,360,543 42	$2,275,012 46	$18,243 34	$2,256,769 12	$1,091 56
Personal Property—					
1903.........	$9,703,850 94	$4,346,835 50	$359 06	$4,346,476 44	$32,553 28
1904.........	....	481,956 67	518 42	481,438 25	....
1905.........	....	86,673 13	392 97	86,280 16	....
1906.........	....	18,445 44	....	18,445 44	....
1907.........	....	2,549 28	....	2,549 28	....
1908.........	....	8,126 41	....	8,126 41	....
1909.........	....	7,853 76	....	7,853 76	....
1910.........	....	624 47	....	624 47	....
1911.........	....	177 83	....	177 83	....
1912.........	....	514 59	....	514 59	....
1913.........	....	1,689 54	....	1,689 54	....
1914.........	....	577 80	....	577 80	....
Totals.	$9,703,850 94	$4,956,024 42	$1,270 45	$4,954,753 97	$32,553 28

Part I-B—Recapitulation—Combining the Four Classes of Tax Shown in the Pre According to Year

Class of Tax and Year of Action.	Amount of Levy.	Collections. Total.	Collections. Less Refunds and Over and Double Payments.	Collections. Net.	Discounts.
Totals for—					
1903.........	$77,631,774 55	$58,133,056 00	$394 80	$58,132,661 20	$398,518 24
1904.........	....	7,579,511 11	59,842 62	7,519,668 49	41 37
1905.........	....	2,027,934 47	11,622 68	2,016,311 79	....
1906.........	....	632,618 75	20,356 32	612,262 43	....
1907.........	....	894,519 67	1,817 64	892,702 03	....
1908.........	....	227,157 27	9,305 62	217,851 65	....
1909.........	....	393,223 00	7,548 59	385,674 41	....
1910.........	....	690,690 12	14,339 32	676,350 80	....
1911.........	....	405,790 16	1,436 37	404,353 79	....
1912.........	....	24,882 50	640 00	24,242 50	....
1913.........	....	47,327 77	1,472 94	45,854 83	....
1914.........	....	9,558 76	1,684 67	7,874 09	....
Grand Totals.	$77,631,774 55	$71,066,269 58	$130,461 57	$70,935,808 01	$398,559 61

Cancellations.	Deductions Under Section 48, Tax Law	Total.	Balance Uncollected at December 31, 1914.	Percentages. Net Collections to Levy.	Percentages. Total Discounts. Cancellations and Deductions to Levy.	Percentages. Un-Collected Balance to Levy.
....	....	$1,091 56	....	....	....	....
....	....	....	....	....	....	....
$3,371 21	....	3,371 21	....	....	....	....
31,229 71	....	31,229 71	....	....	....	....
88,592 03	....	88,592 03	....	....	....	....
....	$31,723 90	31,723 90	....	....	....	....
51,904 50	454,835 15	506,739 65	....	....	....	....
126,150 52	33,761 58	159,912 10	....	....	....	....
206,107 62	19,619 67	225,727 29	....	....	....	....
457 25	....	457 25	....	....	....	....
15,628 12	....	15,628 12	....	....	....	....
1,100 06	....	1,100 06	....	....	....	....
$524,541 02	$539,940 30	$1,065,572 88	$38,201 42	67.16	31.71	1.13
$8,612 87	....	$41,166 15	....	....	....	....
375,870 09	....	375,870 09	....	....	....	....
212,876 54	....	212,876 54	....	....	....	....
22,727 10	....	22,727 10	....	....	....	....
234,049 37	....	234,049 37	....	....	....	....
1,327 41	....	1,327 41	....	....	....	....
148 94	....	148 94	....	....	....	....
1,700 97	....	1,700 97	....	....	....	....
372 35	....	372 35	....	....	....	....
794 46	....	794 46	....	....	....	....
595 76	....	595 76	....	....	....	....
247 89	....	247 89	....	....	....	....
$859,323 75	....	$891,877 03	$3,857,219 94	51.06	9.19	39.75

ceding Part (I-A), and Summarizing the Transactions of the Entire Levy of 1903, *of Occurrence.*

Cancellations.	Deductions Under Section 48, Tax Law	Total.	Balance Uncollected at December 31, 1914.	Net Collections to Levy.	Total Discounts. Cancellations and Deductions to Levy.	Un-Collected Balance to Levy.
$27,966 58	....	$426,484 82	....	74.88	.55	....
439,886 50	....	439,927 87	....	9.68	.57	....
250,625 67	....	250,625 67	....	2.60	.32	....
86,007 78	....	86,007 78	....	.79	.11	....
357,035 00	....	357,035 00	....	1.15	.46	....
11,139 48	31,723 90	42,863 38	....	.28	.05	....
80,410 72	454,835 15	535,245 87	....	.50	.69	....
134,172 81	33,761 58	167,934 39	....	.87	.22	....
215,023 71	19,619 67	234,643 38	....	.52	.30	....
19,911 46	....	19,911 46	....	.03	.03	....
34,530 27	....	34,530 27	....	.06	.04	....
36,751 60	....	36,751 60	....	.01	.05	....
$1,693,461 58	$539,940 30	$2,631,961 49	$4,064,005 05	91.37	3.39	5.24

TABLE VI.—TAX

	Amount of Levy.	Collections. Total.	Less Refunds and Over and Double Payments.	Net.	Discounts.
		Part I.—Classified According to General			
Real Estate (Lands and Buildings)	$72,220,078 07	$71,316,685 51	$190,333 71	$71,126,351 80	$440,231 08
Real Estate of Corporations	495,012 08	458,679 70	105 38	458,574 32	3,611 56
Special Franchise	3,837,072 69	2,664,817 42	28,783 09	2,636,034 33	1,765 40
Personal Property	9,516,240 66	4,972,298 34	2,422 90	4,969,875 44	35,587 65
Grand Totals	$86,068,403 50	$79,412,480 97	$221,645 08	$79,190,835 89	$481,195 69
				Part II.—Classified	
Manhattan	$63,335,951 31	$58,424,497 68	$161,005 41	$58,263,492 27	$376,588 66
The Bronx	4,173,623 51	3,904,770 30	11,286 79	3,893,483 51	20,136 36
Brooklyn	15,579,878 34	14,322,528 05	43,552 96	14,278,975 09	71,735 57
Queens	2,182,720 85	2,046,264 93	5,070 01	2,041,194 92	9,528 17
Richmond	796,229 49	714,420 01	729 91	713,690 10	3,206 93
Grand Totals	$86,068,403 50	$79,412,480 97	$221,645 08	$79,190,835 89	$481,195 69
		Part III.—Classified According to Boroughs			
Manhattan.					
Real Estate (Lands and Buildings)	$52,691,521 37	$52,018,178 21	$142,866 57	$51,875,311 64	$343,294 49
Real Estate of Corporations	79,625 05	64,767 30	....	64,767 30	455 42
Special Franchise	2,874,651 54	2,033,807 55	15,817 42	2,017,990 13	1,290 63
Personal Property	7,690,153 35	4,307,744 62	2,321 42	4,305,423 20	31,548 12
Totals	$63,335,951 31	$58,424,497 68	$161,005 41	$58,263,492 27	$376,588 66
The Bronx.					
Real Estate (Lands and Buildings)	$3,578,294 31	$3,531,003 53	$10,311 24	$3,520,692 29	$18,008 70
Real Estate of Corporations	208,576 75	205,678 60	....	205,678 60	1,838 04
Special Franchise	163,322 10	125,201 03	975 55	124,225 48	109 66
Personal Property	223,430 35	42,887 14	....	42,887 14	179 96
Totals	$4,173,623 51	$3,904,770 30	$11,286 79	$3,893,483 51	$20,136 36
Brooklyn.					
Real Estate (Lands and Buildings)	$13,385,875 39	$13,252,698 13	$32,042 49	$13,220,655 64	$67,570 70
Real Estate of Corporations	112,299 57	98,315 11	105 38	98,209 73	497 39
Special Franchise	688,813 82	431,675 39	11,335 08	420,340 31	284 24
Personal Property	1,392,889 56	539,839 42	70 01	539,769 41	3,383 24
Totals	$15,579,878 34	$14,322,528 05	$43,552 96	$14,278,975 09	$71,735 57
Queens.					
Real Estate (Lands and Buildings)	$1,913,574 62	$1,879,086 70	$4,595 33	$1,874,491 37	$8,637 57
Real Estate of Corporations	65,203 11	61,269 89	....	61,269 89	568 06
Special Franchise	86,421 81	59,968 93	443 21	59,525 72	60 04
Personal Property	117,521 31	45,939 41	31 47	45,907 94	262 50
Totals	$2,182,720 85	$2,046,264 93	$5,070 01	$2,041,194 92	$9,528 17
Richmond.					
Real Estate (Lands and Buildings)	$650,812 38	$635,718 94	$518 08	$635,200 86	$2,719 62
Real Estate of Corporations	29,307 60	28,648 80	....	28,648 80	252 65
Special Franchise	23,863 42	14,164 52	211 83	13,952 69	20 83
Personal Property	92,246 09	35,887 75	....	35,887 75	213 83
Totals	$796,229 49	$714,420 01	$729 91	$713,690 10	$3,206 93

LEVY OF 1904.

Cancellations.	Deductions Under Section 48, Tax Law.	Total.	Balance Uncollected at Dec. 31, 1914.	Percentages. Borough and Specific Levy to Total Levy.	Net Collections to Levy.	Total Discounts, Cancellations and Deductions to Levy.	Uncollected Balance to Levy.
Character of Taxable Property.							
$419,135 28	....	$859,366 36	$234,359 91	83.91	98.49	1.19	.32
18,028 50	....	21,640 06	14,797 70	.57	92.64	4.37	2.99
597,987 45	$560,684 08	1,160,436 93	40,601 43	4.46	68.69	30.25	1.06
205,526 66	....	241,114 31	4,305,250 91	11.06	52.23	2.53	45.24
$1,240,677 89	$560,684 08	$2,282,557 66	$4,595,009 95	100.00	92.01	2.65	5.34
According to Boroughs.							
$989,483 80	$369,248 58	$1,735,321 04	$3,337,138 00	73.59	91.99	2.74	5.27
35,954 32	14,363 99	70,454 67	209,685 33	4.85	93.29	1.69	5.02
201,103 99	177,071 51	449,911 07	850,992 18	18.10	91.65	2.89	5.46
9,149 69	....	18,677 86	122,848 07	2.53	93.52	.85	5.63
4,986 09	....	8,193 02	74,346 37	.93	89.63	1.03	9.34
$1,240,677 89	$560,684 08	$2,282,557 66	$4,595,009 95	100.00	92.01	2.65	5.34
and General Character of Taxable Property.							
$342,255 85	....	$685,550 34	$130,659 39	61.22	98.45	1.30	.25
11,235 57	....	11,690 99	3,166 76	.09	81.34	14.68	3.98
484,657 88	$369,248 58	855,197 09	1,464 32	3.34	70.22	29.75	.05
151,334 50	....	182,882 62	3,201,847 53	8.94	55.99	2.38	41.63
$989,483 80	$369,248 58	$1,735,321 04	$3,337,138 00	73.59	91.99	2.74	5.27
$12,603 77	....	$30,612 47	$26,989 55	4.16	98.39	.86	.75
908 03	....	2,746 07	152 08	.24	98.61	1.32	.07
18,644 07	$14,363 99	33,117 72	5,978 90	.19	76.06	20.28	3.66
3,798 45	....	3,978 41	176,564 80	.26	19.19	1.78	79.03
$35,954 32	$14,363 99	$70,454 67	$209,685 33	4.85	93.29	1.69	5.02
$58,745 75	....	$126,316 45	$38,903 30	15.55	98.77	.94	.29
4,478 16	....	4,975 55	9,114 29	.13	87.45	4.43	8.12
89,682 56	$177,071 51	267,038 31	1,435 20	.80	61.02	38.77	.21
48,197 52	....	51,580 76	801,539 39	1.62	38.75	3.70	57.55
$201,103 99	$177,071 51	$449,911 07	$850,992 18	18.10	91.65	2.89	5.46
$2,986 65	....	$11,624 22	$27,459 03	2.22	97.96	.61	1.43
1,012 52	....	1,580 58	2,352 64	.07	93.97	2.42	3.61
4,351 33	....	4,411 37	22,484 72	.10	68.88	5.10	26.02
799 19	....	1,061 69	70,551 68	.14	39.06	.90	60.04
$9,149 69	....	$8,677 86	$122,848 07	2.53	93.52	.85	5.63
$2,543 26	....	$5,262 88	$10,348 64	.76	97.60	.81	1.59
394 22	....	646 87	11 93	.04	97.75	2.21	.04
651 61	....	672 44	9,238 29	.03	58 47	2.82	38.71
1,397 00	....	1,610 83	54,747 51	.10	38.91	1.74	59.35
$4,986 09	....	$8,193 02	$74,346 37	.93	89.63	1.03	9.34

Part I-A—Tax Levy, 1904, *Supporting and Amplifying Totals Shown in Part I of Classified According to General Character of Taxable Property, and*

Class of Tax and Year of Action.	Amount of Levy.	Collections. Total.	Collections. Less Refunds and Over and Double Payments.	Collections. Net.	Discounts.
Real Estate (Lands and Buildings)—					
1904........	$72,220,078 07	$60,890,721 59	$29 62	$60,890,691 97	$440,231 08
1905........	....	7,332,117 42	62,177 90	7,269,939 52	....
1906........	....	1,549,254 30	6,241 36	1,543,012 94	....
1907........	....	572,460 33	4,311 61	568,148 72	....
1908........	....	301,934 55	32,167 98	269,766 57	....
1909........	....	375,923 21	46,272 82	329,650 39	....
1910........	....	147,907 76	31,914 03	115,993 73	....
1911........	....	74,910 76	1,561 27	73,349 49	....
1912........	....	35,084 88	821 23	34,263 65	....
1913........	....	25,408 23	2,827 03	22,581 20	....
1914........	....	10,962 48	2,008 86	8,953 62	....
Total....	$72,220,078 07	$71,316,685 51	$190,333 71	$71,126,351 80	$440,231 08
Real Estate of Corporations—					
1904........	$495,012 08	$411,384 96	....	$411,384 96	$3,611 56
1905........	....	25,200 71	$78 65	25,122 06	....
1906........	....	3,798 42	....	3,798 42	....
1907........	....	398 61	....	398 61	....
1908........	....	5,791 74	....	5,791 74	....
1909........	....	1,750 23	....	1,750 23	....
1910........	....	7,745 89	26 73	7,719 16	....
1911........	....	877 54	....	877 54	....
1912........	....	1,642 11	....	1,642 11	....
1913........	....	3 02	....	3 02	....
1914........	....	86 47	....	86 47	....
Total....	$495,012 08	$458,679 70	$105 38	$458,574 32	$3,611 56
Special Franchise—					
1904........	$3,837,072 69	$181,205 76	$15,094 63	$166,111 13	$1,765 40
1905........	....	387,661 15	3,273 33	384,387 82	....
1906........	....	72,472 43	9,037 30	63,435 13	....
1907........	....	701,460 15	47 16	701,412 99	....
1908........	....	17,475 58	....	17,475 58	....
1909........	....	141,977 34	....	141,977 34	....
1910........	....	718,690 56	1,330 67	717,359 89	....
1911........	....	413,703 33	....	413,703 33	....
1912........	....	948 53	....	948 53	....
1913........	....	29,222 59	....	29,222 59	....
1914........	....	....	....	....	....
Total....	$3,837,072 69	$2,664,817 42	$28,783 09	$2,636,034 33	$1,765 40
Personal Property—					
1904........	$9,516,240 66	$4,443,571 15	$1,098 70	$4,442,472 45	$35,587 65
1905........	....	433,206 99	424 90	432,782 09	....
1906........	....	66,279 68	....	66,279 68	....
1907........	....	10,526 27	....	10,526 27	....
1908........	....	5,941 86	....	5,941 86	....
1909........	....	9,477 19	....	9,477 19	....
1910........	....	2,163 86	899 30	1,264 56	....

Table VI, Showing All Transactions from October 3, 1904, to December 31, 1914, Further Analyzed According to Year in Which Transactions Were Made.

Cancellations.	Deductions Under Section 48, Tax Law	Total.	Balance Uncollected at December 31, 1914.	Percentages.		
				Net Collections to Levy.	Total Discounts. Cancellations and Deductions to Levy.	Un-Collected Balance to Levy.
$20,649 69	....	$460,880 77	....	....	....	....
60,688 42	....	60,688 42	....	....	....	....
34,893 38	....	34,893 38	....	....	....	....
22,038 62	....	22,038 62	....	....	....	....
46,338 77	....	46,338 77	....	....	....	....
71,493 20	....	71,493 20	....	....	....	....
48,593 71	....	48,593 71	....	....	....	....
15,122 24	....	15,122 24	....	....	....	....
15,110 85	....	15,110 85	....	....	....	....
19,485 22	....	19,485 22	....	....	....	....
64,721 18	....	64,721 18	....	....	....	....
$419,135 28	....	$859,366 36	$234,359 91	98.49	1.19	.32
....	....	$3,611 56	....	....	....	....
$3,106 82	....	3,106 82	....	....	....	....
2,345 80	....	2,345 80	....	....	....	....
912 31	....	912 31	....	....	....	....
....	....	....	....	....	....	....
394 22	....	394 22	....	....	....	....
2,967 10	....	2,967 10	....	....	....	....
....	....	....	....	....	....	....
5,130 98	....	5,130 98	....	....	....	....
....	....	....	....	....	....	....
3,171 27	....	3,171 27	....	....	....	....
$18,028 50	....	$21,640 06	$14,797 70	92.64	4.37	2.99
....	....	$1,765 40	....	....	....	....
$27,795 26	....	27,795 26	....	....	....	....
26,473 86	....	26,473 86	....	....	....	....
98,513 38	....	98,513 38	....	....	....	....
....	$32,313 90	32,313 90	....	....	....	....
43,490 56	482,797 76	526,288 32	....	....	....	....
165,754 45	36,904 55	202,659 00	....	....	....	....
217,673 90	8,667 87	226,341 77	....	....	....	....
401 10	....	401 10	....	....	....	....
16,662 60	....	16,662 60	....	....	....	....
1,222 34	....	1,222 34	....	....	....	....
$597,987 45	$560,684 08	$1,160,436 93	$40,601 43	68.69	30.25	1.06
$10,867 96	....	$46,455 61	....	....	....	....
116,635 19	....	116,635 19	....	....	....	....
25,115 01	....	25,115 01	....	....	....	....
14,433 33	....	14,433 33	....	....	....	....
17,958 89	....	17,958 89	....	....	....	....
3,745 26	....	3,745 26	....	....	....	....
4,552 58	....	4,552 58	....	....	....	....

Class of Tax and Year of Action.	Amount of Levy.	Collections. Total.	Collections. Less Refunds and Over and Double Payments.	Collections. Net.	Discounts.
Personal Property—					
1911.........	....	205 05	....	205 05	....
1912.........	....	46 98	....	46 98	....
1913.........	....	361 08	....	361 08	....
1914.........	....	518 23	....	518 23	....
Total....	$9,516,240 66	$4,972,298 34	$2,422 90	$4,969,875 44	$35,587 65

Part I-B—Recapitulation, Combining the Four Classes of Tax Shown in the Preceding ing to Year of

Totals for—					
1904.........	$86,068,403 50	$65,926,883 46	$16,222 95	$65,910,660 51	$481,195 69
1905.........	....	8,178,186 27	65,954 78	8,112,231 49	....
1906.........	....	1,691,804 83	15,278 66	1,676,526 17	....
1907.........	....	1,284,845 36	4,358 77	1,280,486 59	....
1908.........	....	331,143 73	32,167 98	298,975 75	....
1909.........	....	529,127 97	46,272 82	482,855 15	....
1910.........	....	876,508 07	34,170 73	842,337 34	....
1911.........	....	489,696 68	1,561 27	488,135 41	....
1912.........	....	37,722 50	821 23	36,901 27	....
1913.........	....	54,994 92	2,827 03	52,167 89	....
1914.........	....	11,567 18	2,008 86	9,558 32	....
Grand totals	$86,068,403 50	$79,412,480 97	$221,645 08	$79,190,835 89	$481,195 69

TABLE VII.—TAX

	Amount of Levy.	Collections. Total.	Collections. Less Refunds and Over and Double Payments.	Collections. Net.	Discounts.
			Part I.—Classified	*According*	*to General*
Real Estate (Lands and Buildings)	$73,585,830 65	$72,628,788 97	$209,438 16	$72,419,350 81	$468,956 39
Real Estate of Corporations..	493,042 26	450,195 89	106 19	450,089 70	3,985 53
Special Franchise	4,546,986 43	3,018,412 25	23,685 06	2,994,727 19	3,837 73
Personal Property..........	10,354,826 68	4,791,377 63	100,029 92	4,691,347 71	36,297 77
Grand Totals	$88,980,686 02	$80,888,774 74	$333,259 33	$80,555,515 41	$513,077 42
				Part II.—	*Classified*
Manhattan	$65,407,377 46	$59,196,188 51	$270,006 17	$58,926,182 34	$396,171 59
The Bronx	4,345,274 37	4,035,244 81	12,343 72	4,022,901 09	21,793 82
Brooklyn	16,123,350 54	14,794,701 64	44,039 53	14,750,662 11	81,013 88
Queens	2,324,602 90	2,162,492 49	5,963 28	2,156,529 21	10,706 98
Richmond	780,080 75	700,147 29	906 63	699,240 66	3,391 15
Grand Totals	$88,980,686 02	$80,888,774 74	$333,259 33	$80,555,515 41	$513,077 42
Manhattan.			*Part III.—Classified*	*According*	*to Boroughs*
Real Estate (Lands and Buildings)	$53,469,889 52	$52,772,275 91	$153,580 38	$52,618,695 53	$362,341 51
Real Estate of Corporations..	79,225 42	60,250 12	1 49	60,248 63	467 73
Special Franchise	3,399,167 31	2,257,177 11	18,250 30	2,238,926 81	1,527 70
Personal Property	8,459,095 21	4,106,485 37	98,174 00	4,008,311 37	31,834 65
Totals	$65,407,377 46	$59,196,188 51	$270,006 17	$58,926,182 34	$396,171 59

Cancellations.	Deductions Under Section 48, Tax Law	Total.	Balance Uncollected at December 31, 1914.	Percentages. Net Collections to Levy.	Total Discounts. Cancellations and Deductions to Levy.	Un-Collected Balance to Levy.
925 64	....	925 64	....	....	....	....
4,426 12	....	4,426 12	....	....	....	....
2,300 81	....	2,300 81	....	....	....	....
4,565 87	....	4,565 87	....	....	....	....
$205,526 66	....	$241,114 31	$4,305,250 91	52.23	2.53	45.24

Part (1-A), and Summarizing the Transactions of the Entire Levy of 1904, *According Occurrence.*

$31,517 65	....	$512,713 34	....	....	....	....
208,225 69	....	208,225 69	....	....	....	....
88,828 05	....	88,828 05	....	....	....	....
135,897 64	....	135,897 64	....	....	....	....
64,297 66	$32,313 90	96,611 56	....	....	....	....
119,123 24	482,797 76	601,921 00	....	....	....	....
221,867 84	36,904 55	258,772 39	....	....	....	....
233,721 78	8,667 87	242,389 65	....	....	....	....
25,069 05	....	25,069 05	....	....	....	....
38,448 63	....	38,448 63	....	....	....	....
73,680 66	....	73,680 66	....	....	....	....
$1,240,677 89	$560,684 08	$2,282,557 66	$4,595,009 95	92.01	2.65	5.34

Levy of 1905.

Cancellations.	Deductions Under Section 48, Tax Law.	Total.	Balance Uncollected at Dec. 31, 1914.	Percentages. Borough and Specific Levy to Total Levy.	Net Collections to Levy.	Total Discounts, Cancellations and Deductions to Levy.	Uncollected Balance to Levy.
Character of Taxable Property.							
$401,106 60	....	$870,062 99	$296,416 85	82.70	98.42	1.18	.40
22,182 60	....	26,168 13	16,784 43	.55	91.29	5.31	3.40
913,969 32	$599,032 55	1,516,839 60	35,419 64	5.11	65.87	33.36	.77
1,126,738 04	....	1,163,035 81	4,500,443 16	11.64	45.31	11.23	43.46
$2,463,996 56	$599,032 55	$3,576,106 53	$4,849,064 08	100.00	90.53	4.02	5.45
According to Boroughs.							
$2,015,682 67	$377,158 61	$2,789,012 87	$3,692,182 25	73.50	90.04	4.26	5.70
83,964 05	20,042 41	125,800 28	196,573 00	4.88	92.58	2.90	4.52
336,602 10	201,831 53	619,447 51	753,240 92	18.12	91.49	3.84	4.67
19,988 19	....	30,695 17	137,378 52	2.62	92.77	1.32	5.91
7,759 55	....	11,150 70	69,689 39	.88	89.64	1.43	8.93
$2,463,996 56	$599,032 55	$3,576,106 53	$4,849,064 08	100.00	90.53	4.02	5.45
and General Character of Taxable Property.							
$309,429 84	....	$671,771 35	$179,422 64	60.09	98.40	1.26	.34
15,313 45	....	15,781 18	3,195 61	.09	76.04	19.92	4.04
779,984 95	$377,158 61	1,158,671 26	1,569 24	3.82	65.87	34.09	.04
910,954 43	....	942,789 08	3,507,994 76	9.50	47.38	11.15	41.47
$2,015,682 67	$377,158 61	$2,789,012 87	$3,692,182 25	73.50	90.04	4.26	5.70

	Amount of Levy.	Collections. Total.	Collections. Less Refunds and Over and Double Payments.	Collections. Net.	Discounts.
The Bronx.					
Real Estate (Lands and Buildings)	$3,679,122 76	$3,630,629 45	$10,754 00	$3,619,875 45	$19,587 61
Real Estate of Corporations	207,039 55	205,022 74	....	205,022 74	1,867 03
Special Franchise	210,415 18	155,388 87	1,589 72	153,799 15	140 77
Personal Property	248,696 88	44,203 75	....	44,203 75	198 41
Totals	$4,345,274 37	$4,035,244 81	$12,343 72	$4,022,901 09	$21,793 82
Brooklyn.					
Real Estate (Lands and Buildings)	$13,775,330 38	$13,619,787 92	$38,979 73	$13,580,808 19	$74,495 06
Real Estate of Corporations	112,127 04	97,745 26	104 70	97,640 56	839 22
Special Franchise	815,806 45	520,921 00	3,099 18	517,821 82	1,952 91
Personal Property	1,420,086 67	556,247 46	1,855 92	554,391 54	3,726 69
Totals	$16,123,350 54	$14,794,701 64	$44,039 53	$14,750,662 11	$81,013 88
Queens.					
Real Estate (Lands and Buildings)	$2,020,086 96	$1,980,601 08	$5,532 17	$1,975,068 91	$9,623 98
Real Estate of Corporations	66,183 45	61,458 32	....	61,458 32	582 24
Special Franchise	96,931 08	69,758 93	431 11	69,327 82	192 76
Personal Property	141,401 41	50,674 16	....	50,674 16	308 00
Totals	$2,324,602 90	$2,162,492 49	$5,963 28	$2,156,529 21	$10,706 98
Richmond.					
Real Estate (Lands and Buildings)	$641,401 03	$625,494 61	$591 88	$624,902 73	$2,908 23
Real Estate of Corporations	28,466 80	25,719 45	....	25,719 45	229 31
Special Franchise	24,666 41	15,166 34	314 75	14,851 59	23 59
Personal Property	85,546 51	33,766 89	....	33,766 89	230 02
Totals	$780,080 75	$700,147 29	$906 63	$699,240 66	$3,391 15

Part 1-A—Tax Levy of 1905, Supporting and Amplifying Totals Shown in Part I. of Classified According to General Character of Taxable Property and Fur

Class of Tax and Year of Action.	Amount of Levy.	Collections. Total.	Collections. Less Refunds and Over and Double Payments.	Collections. Net.	Discounts.
Real Estate (Lands and Buildings)—					
1905	$73,585,830 65	$62,970,948 63	$24,332 27	$62,946,616 36	$468,956 39
1906	....	6,964,820 58	72,296 72	6,892,523 86	....
1907	....	1,240,641 79	7,224 65	1,233,417 14	....
1908	....	491,741 38	24,503 76	467,237 62	....
1909	....	564,508 64	21,899 47	542,609 17	....
1910	....	205,902 69	49,613 68	156,289 01	....
1911	....	106,541 33	1,817 16	104,724 17	....
1912	....	40,720 92	2,693 41	38,027 51	....
1913	....	30,458 80	3,087 14	27,371 66	....
1914	....	12,504 21	1,969 90	10,534 31	....
	$73,585,830 65	$72,628,788 97	$209,438 16	$72,419,350 81	$468,956 39

Cancellations.	Deductions Under Section 48, Tax Law.	Total.	Balance Uncollected at Dec. 31, 1914.	Percentages. Borough and Specific Levy to Total Levy.	Net Collections to Levy.	Total Discounts, Cancellations and Deductions to Levy.	Uncollected Balance to Levy.
$11,655 99	....	$31,243 60	$28,003 71	4.13	98.39	.85	.76
59 61	....	1,926 64	90 17	.23	99.03	.93	.04
35,716 51	$20,042 41	55,899 69	716 34	.24	73.09	26.57	.34
36,531 94	....	36,730 35	167,762 78	.28	17.77	14.77	67.46
$83,964 05	$20,042 41	$125,800 28	$196,573 00	4.88	92.58	2.90	4.52
$72,813 65	....	$147,308 71	$47,213 48	15.48	98.58	1.07	.35
5,781 73	....	6,620 95	7,865 53	.13	87.08	5.90	7.02
93,717 38	$201,831 53	297,501 82	482 81	.91	63.47	36.47	.06
164,289 34	....	168,016 03	697,679 10	1.60	39.04	11.83	49.13
$336,602 10	$201,831 53	$619,447 51	$753,240 92	18.12	91.49	3.84	4.67
$4,328 18	....	$13,952 16	$31,065 89	2.27	97.77	.69	1.54
715 39	....	1,297 63	3,427 50	.08	92.86	1.96	5.18
4,264 32	....	4,457 08	23,146 18	.11	71.52	4.60	23.88
10,680 30	....	10,988 30	79,738 95	.16	35.84	7.77	56.39
$19,988 19	....	$30,695 17	$137,378 52	2.62	92.77	1.32	5.91
$2,878 94	....	$5,787 17	$10,711 13	.72	97.43	.90	1.67
312 42	....	541 73	2,205 62	.03	90.35	1.90	7.75
286 16	....	309 75	9,505 07	.03	60.21	1.25	38.54
4,282 03	....	4,512 05	47,267 57	.10	39.50	5.26	55.24
$7,759 55	....	$11,150 70	$69,689 39	.88	89.64	1.43	8.93

Table VII., Showing All Transactions from October 2, 1905, *to December* 31, 1914, *ther Analyzed According to Year in Which Transactions Were Made.*

Cancellations.	Deductions Under Section 48, Tax Law.	Total.	Balance Uncollected at December 31, 1914.	Percentages. Net Collections to Levy.	Total Discounts, Cancellations and Deductions to Levy.	Un-Collected Balance to Levy.
$14,085 73	....	$483,042 12	....	....	....	....
71,683 64	....	71,683 64	....	....	....	....
44,277 45	....	44,277 45	....	....	....	....
35,040 83	....	35,040 83	....	....	....	....
49,958 13	....	49,958 13	....	....	....	....
40,882 50	....	40,882 50	....	....	....	....
36,440 48	....	36,440 48	....	....	....	....
17,002 58	....	17,002 58	....	....	....	....
20,347 37	....	20,347 37	....	....	....	....
71,387 89	....	71,387 89	....	....	....	....
$401,106 60	....	$870,062 99	$296,41[illegible] 85	98.42	1.18	.40

Class of Tax and Year of Action.	Amount of Levy.	Collections. Total.	Less Refunds and Over and Double Payments.	Net.	Discounts.
Real Estate of Corporations—					
1905.........	$493,042 26	$404,440 54	....	$404,440 54	$3,985 53
1906.........	....	9,085 49	$1 49	9,084 00	....
1907.........	....	213 27	78 13	135 14	....
1908.........	....	18,339 85	....	18,339 85	....
1909.........	....	5,429 77	....	5,429 77	....
1910.........	....	10,332 69	26 57	10,306 12	....
1911.........	....	2,250 86	....	2,250 86	....
1912.........	....	18 02	....	18 02	....
1913.........	....	2 98	....	2 98	....
1914.........	....	82 42	....	82 42	....
Totals...	$493,042 26	$450,195 89	$106 19	$450,089 70	$3,985 53
Special Franchise—					
1905.........	$4,546,986 43	$604,444 78	$272 68	$604,172 10	$3,837 73
1906.........	....	104,539 93	21,716 31	82,823 62	....
1907.........	....	798,420 16	90 87	798,329 29	....
1908.........	....	19,859 70	....	19,859 70	....
1909.........	....	159,661 23	....	159,661 23	....
1910.........	....	861,535 88	1,441 90	860,093 98	....
1911.........	....	437,011 29	163 29	436,848 00	....
1912.........	....	1,332 61	....	1,332 61	....
1913.........	....	31,606 67	01	31,606 66	....
1914.........	....	....	....	....	....
Totals...	$4,546,986 43	$3,018,412 25	$23,685 06	$2,994,727 19	$3,837 73
Personal Property—					
1905.........	$10,354,826 68	$4,315,153 52	$97,427 12	$4,217,726 40	$36,297 77
1906.........	....	373,301 55	2,380 70	370,920 85	....
1907.........	....	62,449 96	....	62,449 96	....
1908.........	....	17,162 95	....	17,162 95	....
1909.........	....	16,234 77	....	16,234 77	....
1910.........	....	4,039 48	....	4,039 48	....
1911.........	....	1,878 49	....	1,878 49	....
1912.........	....	670 43	222 10	448 33	....
1913.........	....	181 63	....	181 63	....
1914.........	....	304 85	....	304 85	....
Totals...	$10,354,826 68	$4,791,377 63	$100,029 92	$4,691,347 71	$36,297 77

Part I-B—Recapitulation—Combining the Four Classes of Tax Shown in the Pre According to

Class of Tax and Year of Action.	Amount of Levy.	Total.	Less Refunds and Over and Double Payments.	Net.	Discounts.
Totals for—					
1905.........	$88,980,686 02	$68,294,987 47	$122,032 07	$68,172,955 40	$513,077 42
1906.........	....	7,451,747 55	96,395 22	7,355,352 33	....
1907.........	....	2,101,725 18	7,393 65	2,094,331 53	....
1908.........	....	547,103 88	24,503 76	522,600 12	....
1909.........	....	745,834 41	21,899 47	723,934 94	....
1910.........	....	1,081,810 74	51,082 15	1,030,728 59	....
1911.........	....	547,681 97	1,980 45	545,701 52	....
1912.........	....	42,741 98	2,915 51	39,826 47	....
1913.........	....	62,250 08	3,087 15	59,162 93	....
1914.........	....	12,891 48	1,969 90	10,921 58	....
Grand Totals	$88,980,686 02	$80,888,774 74	$333,259 33	$80,555,515 41	$513,077 42

Cancellations.	Deductions Under Section 48, Tax Law	Total.	Balance Uncollected at December 31, 1914.	Percentages. Net Collections to Levy.	Total Discounts. Cancellations and Deductions to Levy.	Un-Collected Balance to Levy.
$1,322 68	....	$5,308 21	....	....	....	....
292 61	....	292 61	....	....	....	....
....	....	....	....	....	....	....
156 26	....	156 26	....	....	....	....
12,868 00	....	12,868 00	....	....	....	....
2,637 90	....	2,637 90	....	....	....	....
....	....	....	....	....	....	....
2,149 51	....	2,149 51	....	....	....	....
....	....	....	....	....	....	....
2,755 64	....	2,755 64	....	....	....	....
$22,182 60	....	$26,168 13	$16,784 43	91.29	5.31	3.40
$1,146 20	....	$4,983 93	....	....	....	....
53,513 29	....	53,513 29	....	....	....	....
123,822 66	....	123,822 66	....	....	....	....
....	$34,871 55	34,871 55	....	....	....	....
2,471 58	486,434 66	488,906 24	....	....	....	....
487,444 08	43,107 65	530,551 73	....	....	....	....
228,122 27	34,618 69	262,740 96	....	....	....	....
561 76	....	561 76	....	....	....	....
16,887 48	....	16,887 48	....	....	....	....
....	....	....	....	....	....	....
$913,969 32	$599,032 55	$1,516,839 60	$35,419 64	65.87	33.36	.77
$25,695 16	....	$61,992 93	....	....	....	....
459,091 47	....	459,091 47	....	....	....	....
281,380 47	....	281,380 47	....	....	....	....
245,872 55	....	245,872 55	....	....	....	....
34,867 94	....	34,867 94	....	....	....	....
26,497 09	....	26,497 09	....	....	....	....
15,581 82	....	15,581 82	....	....	....	....
13,261 15	....	13,261 15	....	....	....	....
6,556 62	....	6,556 62	....	....	....	....
17,933 77	....	17,933 77	....	....	....	....
$1,126,738 04	....	$1,163,035 81	$4,500,443 16	45.31	11.23	43.46

ceding Part (I-A) and Summarizing the Transactions of the Entire Levy of 1905, *Year of Occurrence.*

Cancellations.	Deductions Under Section 48, Tax Law	Total.	Balance Uncollected at December 31, 1914.	Net Collections to Levy.	Total Discounts. Cancellations and Deductions to Levy.	Un-Collected Balance to Levy.
$42,249 77	....	$555,327 19	....	....	....	....
584,581 01	....	584,581 01	....	....	....	....
449,480 58	....	449,480 58	....	....	....	....
281,069 64	$34,871 55	315,941 19	....	....	....	....
100,165 65	486,434 66	586,600 31	....	....	....	....
557,461 57	43,107 65	600,569 22	....	....	....	....
280,144 57	34,618 69	314,763 26	....	....	....	....
32,975 00	....	32,975 00	....	....	....	....
43,791 47	....	43,791 47	....	....	....	....
92,077 30	....	92,077 30	....	....	....	....
$2,463,996 56	$599,032 55	$3,576,106 53	$4,849,064 08	90.53	4.02	5.45

	Amount of Levy.	Collections. Total.	Collections. Less Refunds and Over and Double Payments.	Collections. Net.	Discounts.
			Part I.—Classified According to General		
Real Estate (Lands and Buildings)	$79,496,876 72	$78,481,879 60	$196,495 90	$78,285,383 70	$489,633 26
Real Estate of Corporations	759,212 75	507,781 88	5,061 87	502,720 01	4,176 80
Special Franchise	5,394,041 11	3,523,477 47	53,579 28	3,469,898 19	873 88
Personal Property	8,444,962 83	4,382,548 74	2,846 85	4,379,701 89	31,668 71
Grand Totals	$94,095,093 41	$86,895,687 69	$257,983 90	$86,637,703 79	$526,352 65
				Part II.—Classified	
Manhattan	$67,320,200 64	$62,213,884 91	$192,414 06	$62,021,470 85	$400,515 94
The Bronx	5,527,934 57	5,133,774 37	16,538 21	5,117,236 16	27,549 69
Brooklyn	17,831,680 77	16,386,684 91	38,760 67	16,347,924 24	82,955 36
Queens	2,629,322 64	2,440,825 09	9,014 15	2,431,810 94	11,812 38
Richmond	785,954 79	720,518 41	1,256 81	719,261 60	3,519 28
Grand Totals	$94,095,093 41	$86,895,687 69	$257,983 90	$86,637,703 79	$526,352 65
			Part III.—Classified According to Boroughs		
Manhattan.					
Real Estate (Lands and Buildings)	$56,528,822 94	$55,804,450 22	$146,077 82	$55,658,372 40	$371,918 06
Real Estate of Corporations	212,989 59	63,413 68	1,205 33	62,208 35	509 00
Special Franchise	3,971,818 51	2,602,518 68	42,659 04	2,559,859 64	448 90
Personal Property	6,606,569 60	3,743,502 33	2,471 87	3,741,030 46	27,639 98
Totals	$67,320,200 64	$62,213,884 91	$192,414 06	$62,021,470 85	$400,515 94
The Bronx.					
Real Estate (Lands and Buildings)	$4,767,853 56	$4,693,984 88	$11,001 31	$4,682,983 57	$24,972 34
Real Estate of Corporations	286,581 45	246,923 28	3,845 14	243,078 14	2,315 25
Special Franchise	206,927 61	140,857 42	1,690 76	139,166 66	47 33
Personal Property	266,571 95	52,008 79	1 00	52,007 79	214 77
Totals	$5,527,934 57	$5,133,774 37	$16,538 21	$5,117,236 16	$27,549 69
Brooklyn.					
Real Estate (Lands and Buildings)	$15,264,914 97	$15,113,511 97	$30,951 40	$15,082,560 57	$78,952 77
Real Estate of Corporations	160,568 26	105,573 22	11 40	105,561 82	512 37
Special Franchise	1,057,741 99	668,802 37	7,440 05	661,362 32	222 10
Personal Property	1,348,455 55	498,797 35	357 82	498,439 53	3,268 12
Totals	$17,831,680 77	$16,386,684 91	$38,760 67	$16,347,924 24	$82,955 36
Queens.					
Real Estate (Lands and Buildings)	$2,276,008 61	$2,227,863 86	$7,698 74	$2,220,165 12	$10,726 15
Real Estate of Corporations	73,040 00	66,298 95	....	66,298 95	609 47
Special Franchise	129,569 33	93,416 26	1,299 85	92,116 41	154 93
Personal Property	150,704 70	53,246 02	15 56	53,230 46	321 83
Totals	$2,629,322 64	$2,440,825 09	$9,014 15	$2,431,810 94	$11,812 38
Richmond.					
Real Estate (Lands and Buildings)	$659,276 64	$642,068 67	$766 63	$641,302 04	$3,063 94
Real Estate of Corporations	26,033 45	25,572 75	....	25,572 75	230 71
Special Franchise	27,983 67	17,882 74	489 58	17,393 16	62
Personal Property	72,661 03	34,994 25	60	34,993 65	224 01
Totals	$785,954 79	$720,518 41	$1,256 81	$719,261 60	$3,519 28

LEVY OF 1906.

Cancellations.	Deductions Under Section 48, Tax Law.	Total.	Balance Uncollected at Dec. 31, 1914.	Percentages. Borough and Specific Levy to Total Levy.	Net Collections to Levy.	Total Discounts, Cancellations and Deductions to Levy.	Uncollected Balance to Levy.
Character of Taxable Property.							
$431,408 56	....	$921,041 82	$290,451 20	84.49	98.48	1.15	.37
236,077 28	....	240,254 08	16,238 66	.81	66.21	31.65	2.14
1,228,506 97	$648,013 68	1,877,394 53	46,748 39	5.73	64.33	34.81	.86
702,532 02	....	734,200 73	3,331,060 21	8.97	51.87	8.69	39.44
$2,598,524 83	$648,013 68	$3,772,891 16	$3,684,498 46	100.00	92.08	4.00	3.92
According to Boroughs.							
$1,984,245 94	$367,707 56	$2,752,469 44	$2,546,260 35	71.55	92.13	4.09	3.78
122,833 96	40,675 26	191,058 91	219,639 50	5.87	92.57	3.46	3.97
458,175 78	239,630 86	780,762 00	702,994 53	18.95	91.68	4.38	3.94
24,218 43	....	36,030 81	161,480 89	2.79	92.49	1.37	6.14
9,050 72	....	12,570 00	54,123 19	.84	91.52	1.59	6.89
$2,598,524 83	$648,013 68	$3,772,891 16	$3,684,498 46	100.00	92.08	4.00	3.92
and General Character of Taxable Property.							
$342,894 76	....	$714,812 82	$155,637 72	60.08	98.46	1.26	.28
146,882 82	....	147,391 82	3,389 42	.23	29.22	69.20	1.59
1,040,139 71	$367,707 56	1,408,296 17	3,662 70	4.22	64.45	35.46	.09
454,328 65	....	481,968 63	2,383,570 51	7.02	56.63	7.29	36.08
$1,984,245 94	$367,707 56	$2,752,469 44	$2,546,260 35	71.55	92.13	4.09	3.78
$13,486 67	....	$38,459 01	$46,410 98	5.07	98.21	.81	.97
41,098 61	....	43,413 86	89 45	.30	84.82	15.15	.03
26,484 36	$40,675 26	67,206 95	554 00	.22	67.25	32.48	.27
41,764 32	....	41,979 09	172,585 07	.28	19.51	15.75	64.74
$122,833 96	$40,675 26	$191,058 91	$219,639 50	5.87	92.57	3.46	3.97
$64,638 85	....	$143,591 62	$38,762 78	16.22	98.81	.94	.25
45,561 56	....	46,073 93	8,932 51	.17	65.74	28.70	5.56
153,502 06	$239,630 86	393,355 02	3,024 65	1.13	62.53	37.19	.28
194,473 31	....	197,741 43	652,274 59	1.43	36.96	14.66	48.38
$458,175 78	$239,630 86	$780,762 00	$702,994 53	18.95	91.68	4.38	3.94
$6,152 58	....	$16,878 73	$38,964 76	2.42	97.55	.74	1.71
2,336 13	....	2,945 60	3,795 45	.08	90.77	4.03	5.20
7,434 87	....	7,589 80	29,863 12	.13	71.09	5.86	23.05
8,294 85	....	8,616 68	88,857 56	.16	35.32	5.72	58.96
$24,218 43	....	$36,030 81	$161,480 89	2.79	92.49	1.37	6.14
$4,235 70	....	$7,299 64	$10,674 96	.70	97.27	1.11	1.62
198 16	....	428 87	31 83	.03	98.23	1.65	.12
945 97	....	946 59	9,643 92	.03	62.16	3.38	34.46
3,670 89	....	3,894 90	33,772 48	.08	48.16	5.36	46.48
$9,050 72	....	$12,570 00	$54,123 19	.84	91.52	1.59	6.89

Part I-A—Tax Levy of 1906, Supporting and Amplifying Totals Shown in Part I Classified According to General Character of Taxable Property, and Further

Class of Tax and Year of Action.	Amount of Levy.	Collections. Total.	Collections. Less Refunds and Over and Double Payments.	Collections. Net.	Discounts.
Real Estate (Lands and Buildings)—					
1906.........	$79,496,876 72	$67,537,418 67	$8,271 87	$67,529,146 80	$489,633 26
1907.........	....	7,783,172 38	74,124 59	7,709,047 79	....
1908.........	....	1,504,988 27	36,248 44	1,468,739 83	....
1909.........	....	895,299 09	25,464 35	869,834 74	....
1910.........	....	390,170 56	20,746 49	369,424 07	....
1911.........	....	209,800 44	20,124 85	189,675 59	....
1912.........	....	72,172 98	4,863 64	67,309 34	....
1913.........	....	65,171 60	3,883 65	61,287 95	....
1914.........	....	23,685 61	2,768 02	20,917 59	....
Total....	$79,496,876 72	$78,481,879 60	$196,495 90	$78,285,383 70	$489,633 26
Real Estate of Corporations—					
1906.........	$759,212 75	$461,169 18	....	$461,169 18	$4,176 80
1907.........	....	6,782 19	$0 03	6,782 16	....
1908.........	....	18,707 95	5,028 26	13,679 69	....
1909.........	....	4,910 17	....	4,910 17	....
1910.........	....	12,380 40	11 40	12,369 00	....
1911.........	....	1,987 06	....	1,987 06	....
1912.........	....	1,625 99	22 18	1,603 81	....
1913.........	....	58 80	....	58 80	....
1914.........	....	160 14	....	160 14	....
Total....	$759,212 75	$507,781 88	$5,061 87	$502,720 01	$4,176 80
Special Franchise—					
1906.........	$5,394,041 11	$639,736 98	$28,349 42	$611,387 56	$873 88
1907.........	....	38,300 79	8,051 76	30,249 03	....
1908.........	....	368,760 45	14 78	368,745 67	....
1909.........	....	734,923 70	500 00	734,423 70	....
1910.........	....	1,107,423 28	3,304 86	1,104,118 42	....
1911.........	....	434,807 01	13,272 27	421,534 74	....
1912.........	....	1,932 29	....	1,932 29	....
1913.........	....	197,592 97	86 19	197,506 78	....
1914.........	....	....	....	....	....
Total....	$5,394,041 11	$3,523,477 47	$53,579 28	$3,469,898 19	$873 88
Personal Property—					
1906.........	$8,444,962 83	$3,859,478 03	$2,818 91	$3,856,659 12	$31,668 71
1907...........	....	433,950 18	10 38	433,939 80	....
1908.........	....	50,494 13	17 56	50,476 57	....
1909.........	....	26,541 50	....	26,541 50	....
1910.........	....	6,735 90	....	6,735 90	....
1911.........	....	1,487 93	....	1,487 93	....
1912.........	....	923 95	....	923 95	....
1913.........	....	2,276 60	....	2,276 60	....
1914.........	....	660 52	....	660 52	....
Total....	$8,444,962 83	$4,382,548 74	$2,846 85	$4,379,701 89	$31,668 71

of Table VIII, Showing All Transactions from October 1, 1906, *to December* 31, 1914, *Analyzed According to Year in Which Transactions Were Made.*

Cancellations.	Deductions Under Section 48, Tax Law.	Total.	Balance Uncollected at December 31, 1914.	Percentages. Net Collections to Levy.	Total Discounts, Cancellations and Deductions to Levy.	Un-Collected Balance to Levy.
$14,294 54	....	$503,927 80	....	....	....	....
94,955 42	....	94,955 42	....	....	....	....
55,926 49	....	55,926 49	....	....	....	....
63,330 83	....	63,330 83	....	....	....	....
28,054 75	....	28,054 75	....	....	....	....
47,968 16	....	47,968 16	....	....	....	....
18,829 05	....	18,829 05	....	....	....	....
21,041 51	....	21,041 51	....	....	....	....
87,007 81	....	87,007 81	....	....	....	....
$431,408 56	....	$921,041 82	$290,451 20	98.48	1.16	.36
$29 57	....	$4,206 37	....	....	....	....
1,282 17	....	1,282 17	....	....	....	....
5,212 78	....	5,212 78	....	....	....	....
52,699 11	....	52,699 11	....	....	....	....
2,611 26	....	2,611 26	....	....	....	....
....	....	....	....	....	....	....
113,947 68	....	113,947 68	....	....	....	....
....	....	....	....	....	....	....
60,294 71	....	60,294 71	....	....	....	....
$236,077 28	....	$240,254 08	$16,238 66	66.22	31.64	2.14
$2,810 20	....	$3,684 08	....	....	....	....
40,972 08	....	40,972 08	....	....	....	....
5,224 48	$41,111 92	46,336 40	....	....	....	....
2,464 76	493,392 81	495,857 57	....	....	....	....
807,007 09	59,844 54	866,851 63	....	....	....	....
260,495 72	53,664 41	314,160 13	....	....	....	....
14,041 11	....	14,041 11	....	....	....	....
93,392 11	....	93,392 11	....	....	....	....
2,099 42	....	2,099 42	....	....	....	....
$1,228,506 97	$648,013 68	$1,877,394 53	$46,748 39	64.33	34.80	.87
$4,537 69	....	$36,206 40	....	....	....	....
69,887 65	....	69,887 65	....	....	....	....
226,509 65	....	226,509 65	....	....	....	....
183,517 05	....	183,517 05	....	....	....	....
92,482 04	....	92,482 04	....	....	....	....
31,681 52	....	31,681 52	....	....	....	....
45,312 19	....	45,312 19	....	....	....	....
9,987 95	....	9,987 95	....	....	....	....
38,616 28	....	38,616 28	....	....	....	....
$702,532 02	....	$734,200 73	$3,331,060 21	51.86	8.69	39.45

Part I-B—Recapitulation, Combining the Four Classes of Tax Shown in the Preced
According to Year

Class of Tax and Year of Action.	Amount of Levy.	Collections.			Discounts.
		Total.	Less Refunds and Over and Double Payments.	Net.	
Totals for—					
1906.........	$94,095,093 41	$72,497,802 86	$39,440 20	$72,458,362 66	$526,352 65
1907.........	....	8,262,205 54	82,186 76	8,180,018 78	....
1908.........	....	1,942,950 80	41,309 04	1,901,641 76	....
1909.........	....	1,661,674 46	25,964 35	1,635,710 11	....
1910.........	....	1,516,710 14	24,062 75	1,492,647 39	....
1911.........	....	648,082 44	33,397 12	614,685 32	....
1912.........	....	76,655 21	4,885 82	71,769 39	....
1913.........	....	265,099 97	3,969 84	261,130 13	....
1914.........	....	24,506 27	2,768 02	21,738 25	....
Grand Totals.	$94,095,093 41	$86,895,687 69	$257,983 90	$86,637,703 79	$526,352 65

Table IX.—Tax

	Amount of Levy.	Collections.			Discounts.
		Total.	Less Refunds and Over and Double Payments.	Net.	
			Part I.—Classified According to General		
Real Estate (Lands and Buildings)	$85,580,422 29	$84,442,505 70	$158,912 42	$84,283,593 28	$448,979 51
Real Estate of Cororations..	1,048,897 83	685,561 17	1,820 72	683,740 45	4,892 06
Special Franchise	7,005,982 97	4,315,559 19	340,507 93	3,975,051 26	6,527 13
Personal Property...........	8,312,366 93	4,504,662 33	1,223 85	4,503,438 48	29,434 10
Grand Totals......	$101,947,670 02	$93,948,288 39	$502,464 92	$93,445,823 47	$489,832 80
					Part II.—Classified
Manhattan	$71,644,241 08	$66,299,921 68	$422,031 33	$65,877,890 35	$368,038 07
The Bronx	6,099,979 08	5,644,968 28	16,985 49	5,627,982 79	25,922 29
Brooklyn	19,799,425 71	17,914,134 99	49,065 27	17,865,069 72	78,900 63
Queens	3,510,026 16	3,257,779 90	12,061 94	3,245,717 96	13,441 47
Richmond	893,997 99	831,483 54	2,320 89	829,162 65	3,530 34
Grand Totals......	$101,947,670 02	$93,948,288 39	$502,464 92	$93,445,823 47	$489,832 80
			Part III.—Classified According to Boroughs		
Manhattan.					
Real Estate (Lands and Buildings)	$59,922,732 62	$59,113,940 24	$110,112 02	$59,003,828 22	$336,786 36
Real Estate of Corporations..	302,538 27	106,346 92	913 26	105,433 66	621 85
Special Franchise	4,994,711 27	3,242,675 64	309,891 85	2,932,783 79	4,936 42
Personal Property	6,424,258 92	3,836,958 88	1,114 20	3,835,844 68	25,693 44
Total	$71,644,241 08	$66,299,921 68	$422,031 33	$65,877,890 35	$368,038 07
The Bronx.					
Real Estate (Lands and Buildings)	$5,193,095 01	$5,107,917 30	$12,392 00	$5,095,525 30	$22,673 66
Real Estate of Corporations..	377,702 82	301,163 22	....	301,163 22	2,562 67
Special Franchise..........	319,584 52	183,978 82	4,592 33	179,386 49	483 40
Personal Property..........	209,596 73	51,908 94	1 16	51,907 78	202 56
Total	$6,099,979 08	$5,644,968 28	$16,985 49	$5,627,982 79	$25,922 29
Brooklyn.					
Real Estate (Lands and Buildings)	$16,659,306 14	$16,513,248 97	$24,964 53	$16,488,284 44	$74,478 67
Real Estate of Corporations..	215,771 33	138,609 29	885 99	137,723 30	598 31

ing Part (I-A), and Summarizing the Transactions of the Entire Levy of 1906 *of Occurrence.*

Cancellations.	Deductions Under Section 48, Tax Law.	Total.	Balance Uncollected at December 31, 1914.	Percentages. Net Collections to Levy.	Percentages. Total Discounts, Cancellations and Deductions to Levy.	Percentages. Un-Collected Balance to Levy.
$21,672 00	....	$548,024 65	....	....	....	....
207,097 32	....	207,097 32	....	....	....	....
292,873 40	$41,111 92	333,985 32	....	....	....	....
302,011 75	493,392 81	795,404 56	....	....	....	....
930,155 14	59,844 54	989,999 68	....	....	....	....
340,145 40	53,664 41	393,809 81	....	....	....	....
192,130 03	....	192,130 03	....	....	....	....
124,421 57	....	124,421 57	....	....	....	....
188,018 22	....	188,018 22	....	....	....	....
$2,598,524 83	$648,013 68	$3,772,891 16	$3,684,498 46	92.08	4.00	3.92

Levy of 1907.

Cancellations.	Deductions Under Section 48, Tax Law.	Total.	Balance Uncollected at Dec. 31, 1914.	Percentages. Borough and Specific Levy to Total Levy.	Percentages. Net Collections to Levy.	Percentages. Total Discounts, Cancellations and Deductions to Levy.	Percentages. Un-collected Balance to Levy.
Character of Taxable Property.							
$480,553 45	....	$929,532 96	$367,296 05	83.95	98.48	1.09	.43
343,201 13	....	348,093 19	17,064 19	1.03	65.19	33.19	1.62
1,906,478 24	$756,770 40	2,669,775 77	361,155 94	8.15	56.74	38.11	5.15
710,195 28	....	739,629 38	3,069,299 07	6.87	54.18	8.89	36.93
$3,440,428 10	$756,770 40	$4,687,031 30	$3,814,815 25	100.00	91.66	4.60	3.74
According to Boroughs.							
$2,624,844 43	$467,526 80	$3,460,409 30	$2,305,941 43	70.28	91.95	4.83	3.22
228,850 23	38,533 29	293,305 81	178,690 48	5.98	92.26	4.81	2.93
530,882 77	250,710 31	860,493 71	1,073,862 28	19.42	90.23	4.35	5.42
40,652 56	....	54,094 03	210,214 17	3.44	92.47	1.54	5.99
15,198 11	....	18,728 45	46,106 89	.88	92.74	2.10	5.16
$3,440,428 10	$756,770 40	$4,687,031 30	$3,814,815 25	100.00	91.66	4.60	3.74
and General Character of Taxable Property.							
$405,560 09	....	$742,346 45	$176,557 95	58.87	98.47	1.24	.29
192,815 05	....	193,436 90	3,667 71	.29	34.85	63.94	1.21
1,586,601 47	$467,526 80	2,059,064 69	2,862 79	4.81	58.72	41.22	.06
439,867 82	....	465,561 26	2,122,852 98	6.31	59.71	7.25	33.04
$2,624,844 43	$467,526 80	$3,460,409 30	$2,305,941 43	70.28	91.95	4.83	3.22
$12,037 42	....	$34,711 08	$62,858 63	5.09	98.12	.67	1.21
73,855 96	....	76,418 63	120 97	.37	79.74	20.23	.03
100,578 02	$38,533 29	139,594 71	603 32	.31	56.13	43.68	.19
42,378 83	....	42,851 39	115,107 56	.21	24.76	20.32	54.92
$228,850 23	$38,533 29	$293,305 81	$178,690 48	5.98	92.26	4.81	2.93
$49,496 49	....	$123,975 16	$47,046 54	16.34	98.97	.75	.28
68,792 74	....	69,391 05	8,656 98	.21	63.83	32.16	4.01

	Amount of Levy.	Collections. Total.	Collections. Less Refunds and Over and Double Payments.	Collections. Net.	Discounts.
Special Franchise...........	1,481,213 71	739,612 08	23,137 03	716,475 05	799 81
Personal Property...........	1,443,134 53	522,664 65	77 72	522,586 93	3,023 84
Total	$19,799,425 71	$17,914,134 99	$49,065 27	$17,865,069 72	$78,900 63
Queens.					
Real Estate (Lands and Buildings)	$3,035,745 88	$2,959,523 57	$9,899 55	$2,949,624 02	$11,976 76
Real Estate of Corporations..	123,177 62	112,302 37	21 47	112,280 90	878 33
Special Franchise...........	179,449 71	129,422 93	2,110 15	127,312 78	261 70
Personal Property...........	171,652 95	56,531 03	30 77	56,500 26	324 68
Total	$3,510,026 16	$3,257,779 90	$12,061 94	$3,245,717 96	$13,441 47
Richmond.					
Real Estate (Lands and Buildings)	$769,542 64	$747,875 62	$1,544 32	$746,331 30	$3,064 06
Real Estate of Corporations..	29,707 79	27,139 37	....	27,139 37	230 90
Special Franchise............	31,023 76	19,869 72	776 57	19,093 15	45 80
Personal Property...........	63,723 80	36,598 83	....	36,598 83	189 58
Total	$893,997 99	$831,483 54	$2,320 89	$829,162 65	$3,530 34

Part I-A—Tax Levy of 1907, Supporting and Amplifying Totals Shown in Part I. of Classified According to General Character of Taxable Property, and Fur

Class of Tax and Year of Action.	Amount of Levy.	Collections. Total.	Collections. Less Refunds and Over and Double Payments.	Collections. Net.	Discounts.
Real Estate (Lands and Buildings)—					
1907.........	$85,580,422 29	$67,455,227 99	$2,743 32	$67,452,484 67	$448,939 83
1908.........	....	12,806,819 28	69,042 81	12,737,776 47	39 68
1909.........	....	2,505,917 23	40,738 58	2,465,178 65	....
1910.........	....	899,948 68	9,274 25	890,674 43	....
1911.........	....	389,471 44	20,362 79	369,108 65	....
1912.........	....	186,528 71	6,219 24	180,309 47	....
1913.........	....	152,786 23	6,825 97	145,960 26	....
1914.........	....	45,806 14	3,705 46	42,100 68	....
Totals...	$85,580,422 29	$84,442,505 70	$158,912 42	$84,283,593 28	$448,979 51
Real Estate of Corporations—					
1907.........	$1,048 897 83	$543,547 31	....	$543,547 31	$4,892 06
1908.........	....	91,830 42	$21 47	91,808 95	....
1909.........	....	28,026 54	....	28,026 54	....
1910.........	....	7,837 47	885 99	6,951 48	....
1911.........	....	1,948 86	....	1,948 86	....
1912.........	....	1,701 82	22 27	1,679 55	....
1913.........	....	2,994 50	890 99	2,103 51	....
1914.........	....	7,674 25	....	7,674 25	....
Totals...	$1,048,897 83	$685,561 17	$1,820 72	$683,740 45	$4,892 06
Special Franchise—					
1907.........	$7,005,982 97	$787,924 82	$776 57	$787,148 25	$6,527 13
1908.........	....	583,023 07	17,338 63	565,684 44	....
1909.........	....	794,067 34	....	794,067 34	....

Cancellations.	Deductions Under Section 48, Tax Law.	Total.	Balance Uncollected at Dec. 31, 1914.	Percentages.			
				Borough and Specific Levy to Total Levy.	Net Collections to Levy.	Total Discounts, Cancellations and Deductions to Levy.	Un-collected Balance to Levy.
201,623 74	$250,710 31	453,133 86	311,604 80	1.45	48.37	30.59	21.04
210,969 80	....	213,993 64	706,553 96	1.42	36.21	14.83	48.96
$530,882 77	$250,710 31	$860,493 71	$1,073,862 28	19.42	90.23	4.35	5.42
$6,531 60	....	$18,508 36	$67,613 50	2.97	97.16	.61	2.23
5,466 51	....	6,344 84	4,551 88	.12	91.15	5.15	3.70
16,403 38	....	16,665 08	35,471 85	.18	70.95	9.29	19.76
12,251 07	....	12,575 75	102,576 94	.17	32.92	7.33	59.75
$40,652 56	....	$54,094 03	$210,214 17	3.44	92.47	1.54	5.99
$6,927 85	....	$9,991 91	$13,219 43	.76	96.98	1.30	1.72
2,270 87	....	2,501 77	66 65	.03	91.35	8.42	.23
1,271 63	....	1,317 43	10,613 18	.03	61.54	4.25	34.21
4,727 76	....	4,917 34	22,207 63	.06	57.43	7.72	34.85
$15,198 11	....	$18,728 45	$46,106 89	.88	92.74	2.10	5.16

Table IX., Showing All Transactions from October 7, 1907, to December 31, 1914, ther Analyzed According to Year in Which Transactions Were Made.

Cancellations.	Deductions Under Section 48, Tax Law.	Total.	Balance Uncollected at December 31, 1914.	Percentages.		
				Net Collections to Levy.	Total Discounts, Cancellations and Deductions to Levy.	Un-Collected Balance to Levy.
$13,629 88	....	$462,569 71	....	....	....	....
177,312 87	....	177,352 55	....	....	....	....
65,288 26	....	65,288 26	....	....	....	....
12,217 87	....	12,217 87	....	....	....	....
22,017 30	....	22,017 30	....	....	....	....
29,180 04	....	29,180 04	....	....	....	....
34,604 43	....	34,604 43	....	....	....	....
126,302 80	....	126,302 80	....	....	....	....
$480,553 45	....	$929,532 96	$367,296 05	98.48	1.09	.43
$24,510 10	....	$29,402 16	....	....	....	....
186 48	....	186 48	....	....	....	....
52,951 63	....	52,951 63	....	....	....	....
87,640 49	....	87,640 49	....	....	....	....
854 74	....	854 74	....	....	....	....
114,768 99	....	114,768 99	....	....	....	....
1,471 95	....	1,471 95	....	....	....	....
60,816 75	....	60,816 75	....	....	....	....
$343,201 13	....	$348,093 19	$17,064 19	65.19	33.19	1.62
$178 19	....	$6,705 32	....	....	....	....
20,706 20	$45,777 66	66,483 86	....	....	....	....
362,439 99	605,140 24	967,580 23	....	....	....	....

Class of Tax and Year of Action.	Amount of Levy.	Collections. Total.	Less Refunds and Over and Double Payments.	Net.	Discounts.
Special Franchise—					
1910.........	....	1,394,035 56	12,031 69	1,382,003 87	....
1911.........	....	578,053 18	300,929 61	277,123 57	....
1912.........	....	2,096 62	1,366 19	730 43	....
1913.........	....	176,358 60	8,065 24	168,293 36	....
1914.........	....	....	....	....	....
Totals...	$7,005,982 97	$4,315,559 19	$340,507 93	$3,975,051 26	$6,527 13
Personal Property—					
1907.........	$8,312,366 93	$3,934,711 53	$867 24	$3,933,844 29	$29,434 10
1908.........	....	472,010 67	108 49	471,902 18	....
1909.........	....	66,884 52	42 01	66,842 51	....
1910.........	....	18,569 81	1 16	18,568 65	....
1911.........	....	5,479 17	....	5,479 17	....
1912.........	....	3,214 65	....	3,214 65	....
1913.........	....	2,715 04	....	2,715 04	....
1914.........	....	1,076 94	204 95	871 99	....
Totals...	$8,312,366 93	$4,504,662 33	$1,223 85	$4,503,438 48	$29,434 10

Part I-B—Recapitulation, Combining the Four Classes of Tax Shown in the Prece According to Year

Totals for—					
1907.........	$101,947,670 02	$72,721,411 65	$4,387 13	$72,717,024 52	$489,793 12
1908.........	....	13,953,683 44	86,511 40	13,867,172 04	39 68
1909.........	....	3,394,895 63	40,780 59	3,354,115 04	....
1910.........	....	2,320,391 52	22,193 09	2,298,198 43	....
1911.........	....	974,952 65	321,292 40	653,660 25	....
1912.........	....	193,541 80	7,607 70	185,934 10	....
1913.........	....	334,854 37	15,782 20	319,072 17	....
1914.........	....	54,557 33	3,910 41	50,646 92	....
Grand Totals..	$101,947,670 02	$93,948,288 39	$502,464 92	$93,445,823 47	$489,832 80

TABLE X.—TAX

	Amount of Levy.	Collections. Total.	Less Refunds and Over and Double Payments.	Net.	Discounts.
Part I.—Classified According to General					
Real Estate (Lands and Buildings)	$99,989,581 80	$99,206,074 63	$209,753 43	$98,996,321 20	....
Real Estate of Corporations..	1,445,418 58	838,262 94	9,164 36	829,098 58	....
Special Franchise	8,017,257 50	4,890,706 11	270,466 95	4,620,239 16	....
Personal Property	7,088,825 73	4,366,205 67	1,422 98	4,364,782 69	....
Grand Totals.......	**$116,541,083 61**	**$109,301,249 35**	**$490,807 72**	**$108,810,441 63**	....
Part II.—Classified					
Manhattan	$79,288,132 78	$75,046,548 59	$341,140 49	$74,705,408 10	....
The Bronx	7,308,571 04	6,899,483 77	18,728 68	6,880,755 09	....
Brooklyn	23,687,886 38	21,532,781 54	103,641 58	21,429,139 96	....
Queens	5,086,297 55	4,709,488 51	23,393 95	4,686,094 56	....
Richmond	1,170,195 86	1,112,946 94	3,903 02	1,109,043 92	....
Grand Totals.......	**$116,541,083 61**	**$109,301,249 35**	**$490,807 72**	**$108,810,441 63**	....

Cancellations.	Deductions Under Section 48, Tax Law.	Total.	Balance Uncollected at December 31, 1914.	Percentages. Net Collections to Levy.	Total Discounts, Cancellations and Deductions to Levy.	Un-Collected Balance to Levy.
730,164 84	47,854 49	778,019 33	....	....	....	....
360,658 49	57,998 01	418,656 50	....	....	....	....
261,071 44	....	261,071 44	....	....	....	....
168,905 64	....	168,905 64	....	....	....	....
2,353 45	....	2,353 45	....	....	....	....
$1,906,478 24	$756,770 40	$2,669,775 77	$361,155 94	56.74	38.11	5.15
$9,281 02	....	$38,715 12	....	....	....	....
40,389 77	....	40,389 77	....	....	....	....
193,801 72	....	193,801 72	....	....	....	....
274,462 87	....	274,462 87	....	....	....	....
58,894 56	....	58,894 56	....	....	....	....
78,551 69	....	78,551 69	....	....	....	....
9,714 15	....	9,714 15	....	....	....	....
45,099 50	....	45,099 50	....	....	....	....
$710,195 28	....	$739,629 38	$3,069,299 07	54.18	8.89	36.93

ding Part (I-A), and Summarizing the Transactions of the Entire Levy of 1907 *of Occurrence.*

Cancellations.	Deductions Under Section 48, Tax Law.	Total.	Balance Uncollected at December 31, 1914.	Net Collections to Levy.	Total Discounts, Cancellations and Deductions to Levy.	Un-Collected Balance to Levy.
$47,599 19	....	$537,392 31	....	71.34	.53	....
238,595 32	$45,777 66	284,412 66	....	13.60	.28	....
674,481 60	605,140 24	1,279,621 84	....	3.29	1.25	....
1,104,486 07	47,854 49	1,152,340 56	....	2.25	1.13	....
442,425 09	57,998 01	500,423 10	....	.64	.49	....
483,572 16	....	483,572 16	....	.18	.47	....
214,696 17	....	214,696 17	....	.31	.21	....
234,572 50	....	234,572 50	....	.05	.24	....
$3,440,428 10	$756,770 40	$4,687,031 30	$3,814,815 25	91.66	4.60	3.74

Levy of 1908.

Cancellations.	Deductions Under Section 48, Tax Law.	Total.	Balance Uncollected at Dec. 31, 1914.	Percentages. Borough and Specific Levy to Total Levy.	Net Collections to Levy.	Total Discounts, Cancellations and Deductions to Levy.	Un-collected Balance to Levy.
Character of Taxable Property.							
$468,653 98	....	$468,653 98	$524,606 62	85.80	99.01	.47	.52
601,616 90	....	601,616 90	14,703 10	1.24	57.37	41.62	1.01
2,017,443 90	$880,772 34	2,898,216 24	498,802 10	6.88	57.63	36.15	6.22
559,066 49	....	559,066 49	2,164,976 55	6.08	61.58	7.88	30.54
$3,646,781 27	$880,772 34	$4,527,553 61	$3,203,088 37	100.00	93.37	3.88	2.75
According to Boroughs.							
$2,643,494 44	$562,934 54	$3,206,428 98	$1,376,295 70	68.04	94.23	4.04	1.73
222,232 40	14,862 87	237,095 27	190,720 68	6.27	94.15	3.24	2.61
677,394 92	301,358 85	978,753 77	1,279,992 65	20.33	90.46	4.13	5.41
89,875 70	1,616 08	91,491 78	308,711 21	4.36	92.13	1.80	6.07
13,783 81	....	13,783 81	47,368 13	1.00	94.77	1.18	4.05
$3,646,781 27	$880,772 34	$4,527,553 61	$3,203,088 37	100.00	93.37	3.88	2.75

Part III.—Classified According to Boroughs

	Amount of Levy.	Collections. Total.	Collections. Less Refunds and Over and Double Payments.	Collections. Net.	Discounts.
Manhattan.					
Real Estate (Lands and Buildings)	$67,914,140 95	$67,546,954 72	$147,364 22	$67,399,590 50	....
Real Estate of Corporations..	489,124 14	133,656 40	8,312 46	125,343 94	....
Special Franchise	5,593,868 83	3,587,703 12	185,047 49	3,402,655 63	....
Personal Property	5,290,998 86	3,778,234 35	416 32	3,777,818 03	....
Totals	$79,288,132 78	$75,046,548 59	$341,140 49	$74,705,408 10	....
The Bronx.					
Real Estate (Lands and Buildings)	$6,328,158 89	$6,232,954 41	$13,055 95	$6,219,898 46	....
Real Estate of Corporations..	412,228 93	353,652 85	09	353,652 76	....
Special Franchise	381,086 60	264,124 93	5,672 64	258,452 29	....
Personal Property	187,096 62	48,751 58	....	48,751 58	....
Totals	$7,308,571 04	$6,899,483 77	$18,728 68	$6,880,755 09	....
Brooklyn.					
Real Estate (Lands and Buildings)	$20,213,477 98	$20,058,154 32	$27,537 85	$20,030,616 47	....
Real Estate of Corporations..	345,322 64	182,381 59	851 81	181,529 78	....
Special Franchise	1,735,350 27	831,701 80	74,792 81	756,908 99	....
Personal Property	1,393,735 49	460,543 83	459 11	460,084 72	....
Totals	$23,687,886 38	$21,532,781 54	$103,641 58	$21,429,139 96	....
Queens.					
Real Estate (Lands and Buildings)	$4,494,782 94	$4,354,344 46	$20,382 23	$4,333,962 23	....
Real Estate of Corporations..	162,980 77	135,319 38	....	135,319 38	....
Special Franchise	264,023 40	176,461 42	3,011 72	173,449 70	....
Personal Property	164,510 44	43,363 25	....	43,363 25	....
Totals	$5,086,297 55	$4,709,488 51	$23,393 95	$4,686,094 56	....
Richmond.					
Real Estate (Lands and Buildings)	$1,039,021 04	$1,013,666 72	$1,413 18	$1,012,253 54	....
Real Estate of Corporations..	35,762 10	33,252 72	....	33,252 72	....
Special Franchise	42,928 40	30,714 84	1,942 29	28,772 55	....
Personal Property	52,484 32	35,312 66	547 55	34,765 11	....
Totals	$1,170,195 86	$1,112,946 94	$3,903 02	$1,109,043 92	....

Part I-A—Tax Levy of 1908, *Supporting and Amplifying Totals Shown in Part I Classified According to General Character of Taxable Property, and Further*

Class of Tax and Year of Action.	Amount of Levy.	Collections. Total.	Collections. Less Refunds and Over and Double Payments.	Collections. Net.	Discounts.
Real Estate (Lands and Buildings)—					
1908	$99,989,581 80	$80,651,701 45	$2,556 56	$80,649,144 89	....
1909	....	14,029,091 13	130,965 62	13,898,125 51	....
1910	....	2,554,814 83	27,127 18	2,527,687 65	....
1911	....	969,415 25	24,731 96	944,683 29	....
1912	....	469,540 42	11,269 57	458,270 85	....
1913	....	396,042 04	6,226 39	389,815 65	....
1914	....	135,469 51	6,876 15	128,593 36	....
Total....	$99,989,581 80	$99,206,074 63	$209,753 43	$98,996,321 20	....

Cancellations.	Deductions Under Section 48, Tax Law.	Total.	Balance Uncollected at Dec. 31, 1914.	Percentages. Borough and Specific Levy to Total Levy.	Net Collections to Levy.	Total Discounts, Cancellations and Deductions to Levy.	Uncollected Balance to Levy.
and General Character of Taxable Property.							
$344,017 82	....	$344,017 82	$170,532 63	58.28	99.24	.51	.25
363,013 63	....	363,013 63	766 57	.42	25.63	74.21	.16
1,597,921 09	$562,934 54	2,160,855 63	30,357 57	4.80	60.83	38.63	.54
338,541 90	....	338,541 90	1,174,638 93	4.54	71.40	6.40	22.20
$2,643,494 44	$562,934 54	$3,206,428 98	$1,376,295 70	68.04	94.23	4.04	1.73
$18,135 01	....	$18,135 01	$90,125 42	5.43	98.29	.29	1.42
58,469 66	....	58,469 66	106 51	.35	85.80	14.18	.02
107,090 23	$14,862 87	121,953 10	681 21	.33	67.82	32.00	.18
38,537 50	....	38,537 50	99,807 54	.16	26.06	20.59	53.35
$222,232 40	$14,862 87	$237,095 27	$190,720 68	6.27	94.15	3.24	2.61
$77,345 82	....	$77,345 82	$105,515 69	17.35	99.10	.38	.52
154,709 82	....	154,709 82	9,083 04	.29	52.27	44.80	2.63
277,485 15	$301,358 85	578,844 00	399,597 28	1.50	43.62	33.35	23.03
167,854 13	....	167,854 13	765,796 64	1.19	33.01	12.04	54.95
$677,394 92	$301,358 85	$978,753 77	$1,279,992 65	20.33	90.46	4.13	5.41
$23,128 07	....	$23,128 07	$137,692 64	3.85	96.42	.51	3.07
22,976 00	....	22,976 00	4,685 39	.14	83.03	14.10	2.87
32,386 32	$1,616 08	34,002 40	56,571 30	.23	65.69	12.88	21.43
11,385 31	....	11,385 31	109,761 88	.14	26.36	6.92	66.72
$89,875 70	$1,616 08	$91,491 78	$308,711 21	4.36	92.13	1.80	6.07
$6,027 26	....	$6,027 26	$20,740 24	.88	97.42	.58	2.00
2,447 79	....	2,447 79	61 59	.03	92.99	6.84	.17
2,561 11	....	2,561 11	11,594 74	.04	67.02	5.97	27.01
2,747 65	....	2,747 65	14,971 56	.05	66.24	5.23	28.53
$13,783 81	....	$13,783 81	$47,368 13	1.00	94.77	1.18	4.05

of Table X, Showing All Transactions from October 5, 1908, *to December* 31, 1914, *Analyzed According to Year in Which Transactions were Made.*

Cancellations.	Deductions Under Section 48, Tax Law.	Total.	Balance Uncollected at December 31, 1914.	Percentages. Net Collections to Levy.	Total Discounts, Cancellations and Deductions to Levy.	Un-Collected Balance to Levy.
$27,854 34	....	$27,854 34	....	....	....	....
148,683 25	....	148,683 25	....	....	....	....
35,048 90	....	35,048 90	....	....	....	....
28,940 56	....	28,940 56	....	....	....	....
29,661 56	....	29,661 56	....	....	....	....
57,973 44	....	57,973 44	....	....	....	....
140,491 93	....	140,491 93	....	....	....	....
$468,653 98	....	$468,653 98	$524,606 62	99.01	.47	.52

Class of Tax and Year of Action.	Amount of Levy.	Collections. Total.	Collections. Less Refunds and Over and Double Payments.	Collections. Net.	Discounts.
Real Estate of Corporations—					
1908.........	$1,445,418 58	$743,835 88	....	$743,835 88	....
1909.........	....	10,755 26	$8,312 46	2,442 80	....
1910.........	....	10,110 21	851 81	9,258 40	....
1911.........	....	719 55	....	719 55	....
1912.........	....	1,597 12	09	1,597 03	....
1913.........	....	70,127 70	....	70,127 70	....
1914.........	....	1,117 22	....	1,117 22	....
Total....	$1,445,418 58	$838,262 94	$9,164 36	$829,098 58	....
Special Franchise—					
1908.........	$8,017,257 50	$786,485 77	....	$786,485 77	....
1909.........	....	1,606,493 36	$0 01	1,606,493 35	....
1910.........	....	1,518,554 55	145,977 40	1,372,577 15	....
1911..........	....	622,006 61	124,463 72	497,542 89	....
1912.........	....	12,850 56	....	12,850 56	....
1913.........	....	344,298 15	25 82	344,272 33	....
1914.........	....	17 11	....	17 11	....
Total.....	$8,017,257 50	$4,890,706 11	$270,466 95	$4,620,239 16	....
Personal Property—					
1908.........	$7,088,825 73	$3,867,752 07	$551 41	$3,867,200 66	....
1909.........	....	444,587 86	871 57	443,716 29	....
1910.........	....	40,915 84	....	40,915 84	....
1911.........	....	8,271 20	....	8,271 20	....
1912.........	....	1,301 05	....	1,301 05	....
1913.........	....	1,845 14	....	1,845 14	....
1914.........	....	1,532 51	....	1,532 51	....
Total.....	$7,088,825 73	$4,366,205 67	$1,422 98	$4,364,782 69	....

Part I-B—Recapitulation, Combining the Four Classes of Tax Shown in the Preced ing to Year

Class of Tax and Year of Action.	Amount of Levy.	Total.	Less Refunds and Over and Double Payments.	Net.	Discounts.
Totals for—					
1908.........	$116,541,083 61	$86,049,775 17	$3,107 97	$86,046,667 20	....
1909.........	....	16,090,927 61	140,149 66	15,950,777 95	....
1910.........	....	4,124,395 43	173,956 39	3,950,439 04	....
1911.........	....	1,600,412 61	149,195 68	1,451,216 93	....
1912.........	....	485,289 15	11,269 66	474,019 49	....
1913.........	....	812,313 03	6,252 21	806,060 82	....
1914.........	....	138,136 35	6,876 15	131,260 20	....
Grand Totals..	$116,541,083 61	$109,301,249 35	$490,807 72	$108,810,441 63	....

Cancellations.	Deductions Under Section 48, Tax Law.	Total.	Balance Uncollected at December 31, 1914.	Percentages. Net Collections to Levy.	Total Discounts, Cancellations and Deductions to Levy.	Un-Collected Balance to Levy.
$6,140 02	....	$6,140 02	....	....	....	....
345,393 33	....	345,393 33	....	....	....	....
3,102 26	....	3,102 26	....	....	....	....
835 10	....	835 10	....	....	....	....
142,526 48	....	142,526 48	....	....	....	....
34,822 17	....	34,822 17	....	....	....	....
68,797 54	....	68,797 54	....	....	....	....
$601,616 90	....	$601,616 90	$14,703 10	57.37	41.62	1.01
$342 17	$1,665 08	$2,007 25	....	....	....	....
393,963 57	649,707 39	1,043,670 96	....	....	....	....
798,642 57	201,601 96	1,000,244 53	....	....	....	....
418,313 80	20,978 84	439,292 64	....	....	....	....
245,851 41	6,389 74	252,241 15	....	....	....	....
157,637 87	25 82	157,663 69	....	....	....	....
2,692 51	403 51	3,096 02	....	....	....	....
$2,017,443 90	$880,772 34	$2,898,216 24	$498,802 10	57.63	36.15	6.22
$6,395 09	....	$6,395 09	....	....	....	....
27,035 91	....	27,035 91	....	....	....	....
235,430 94	....	235,430 94	....	....	....	....
104,306 64	....	104,306 64	....	....	....	....
161,436 83	....	161,436 83	....	....	....	....
19,949 84	....	19,949 84	....	....	....	....
4,511 24	....	4,511 24	....	....	....	....
$559,066 49	....	$559,066 49	$2,164,976 55	61.58	7.88	30.54

ing Part (I-A), and Summarizing the Transactions of the Entire Levy of 1908 *According of Occurrence.*

$40,731 62	$1,665 08	$42,396 70	....	73.83	.04	....
915,076 06	649,707 39	1,564,783 45	....	13.69	1.34	....
1,072,224 67	201,601 96	1,273,826 63	....	3.39	1.09	....
552,396 10	20,978 84	573,374 94	....	1.25	.49	....
579,476 28	6,389 74	585,866 02	....	.41	.50	....
270,383 32	25 82	270,409 14	....	.69	.23	....
216,493 22	403 51	216,896 73	....	.11	.19	....
$3,646,781 27	$880,772 34	$4,527,553 61	$3,203,088 37	93.37	3.88	2.75

TABLE XI.—TAX

	Amount of Levy.	Collections. Total.	Less Refunds and Over and Double Payments.	Net.	Discounts.
			Part I.—Classified According to General		
Real Estate (Lands and Buildings)	$105,933,728 87	$105,021,603 22	$137,015 72	$104,884,587 50	....
Real Estate of Corporations	1,289,192 17	1,034,902 00	151 02	1,034,750 98	....
Special Franchise	8,022,692 92	5,054,876 78	218,361 86	4,836,514 92	....
Personal Property	7,497,019 70	4,556,648 22	1,559 03	4,555,089 19	....
Grand Totals	$122,742,633 66	$115,668,030 22	$357,087 63	$115,310,942 59	....
				Part II.—Classified	
Manhattan	$83,006,212 80	$79,064,213 57	$306,620 20	$78,757,593 37	....
The Bronx	7,998,343 88	7,433,446 36	10,811 11	7,422,635 25	....
Brooklyn	25,008,502 11	22,925,288 60	21,367 22	22,903,921 38	....
Queens	5,482,432 25	5,086,807 80	14,437 77	5,072,370 03	....
Richmond	1,247,142 62	1,158,273 89	3,851 33	1,154,422 56	....
Grand Totals	$122,742,633 66	$115,668,030 22	$357,087 63	$115,310,942 59	....
		Part III.—Classified According to Boroughs			
Manhattan.					
Real Estate (Lands and Buildings)	$71,526,892 43	$71,152,577 35	$91,169 26	$71,061,408 09	....
Real Estate of Corporations	295,223 92	149,842 10	151 02	149,691 08	....
Special Franchise	5,609,683 82	3,790,866 50	213,928 44	3,576,938 06	....
Personal Property	5,574,412 63	3,970,927 62	1,371 48	3,969,556 14	....
Totals	$83,006,212 80	$79,064,213 57	$306,620 20	$78,757,593 37	....
The Bronx.					
Real Estate (Lands and Buildings)	$6,884,680 47	$6,722,529 76	$9,597 06	$6,712,932 70	....
Real Estate of Corporations	489,959 47	454,262 55	....	454,262 55	....
Special Franchise	389,462 84	209,048 01	1,214 05	207,833 96	....
Personal Property	234,241 10	47,606 04	....	47,606 04	....
Totals	$7,998,343 88	$7,433,446 36	$10,811 11	$7,422,635 25	....
Brooklyn.					
Real Estate (Lands and Buildings)	$21,543,038 32	$21,392,772 70	$20,206 00	$21,372,566 70	....
Real Estate of Corporations	279,946 88	218,590 29	....	218,590 29	....
Special Franchise	1,720,013 07	858,186 13	1,042 68	857,143 45	....
Personal Property	1,465,503 84	455,739 48	118 54	455,620 94	....
Totals	$25,008,502 11	$22,925,288 60	$21,367 22	$22,903,921 38	....
Queens.					
Real Estate (Lands and Buildings)	$4,872,894 77	$4,690,960 86	$13,751 94	$4,677,208 92	....
Real Estate of Corporations	185,971 98	177,747 44	....	177,747 44	....
Special Franchise	256,676 35	174,010 85	616 82	173,394 03	....
Personal Property	166,889 15	44,088 65	69 01	44,019 64	....
Totals	$5,482,432 25	$5,086,807 80	$14,437 77	$5,072,370 03	....
Richmond.					
Real Estate (Lands and Buildings)	$1,106,222 88	$1,062,762 55	$2,291 46	$1,060,471 09	....
Real Estate of Corporations	38,089 92	34,459 62	....	34,459 62	....
Special Franchise	46,856 84	22,765 29	1,559 87	21,205 42	....
Personal Property	55,972 98	38,286 43	....	38,286 43	....
Totals	$1,247,142 62	$1,158,273 89	$3,851 33	$1,154,422 56	....

LEVY OF 1909.

Cancellations.	Deductions Under Section 48, Tax Law.	Total.	Balance Uncollected at Dec. 31, 1914.	Percentages. Borough and Specific Levy to Total Levy.	Net Collections to Levy.	Total Discounts, Cancellations and Deductions to Levy.	Uncollected Balance to Levy.
Character of Taxable Property.							
$355,533 35	....	$355,533 35	$693,608 02	86.30	99.01	.33	.66
233,231 69	....	233,231 69	21,209 50	1.05	80.27	18.09	1.64
2,077,676 06	$982,870 12	3,060,546 18	125,631 82	6.54	60.29	38.15	1.56
552,205 17	....	552,205 17	2,389,725 34	6.11	60.76	7.37	31.87
$3,218,646 27	$982,870 12	$4,201,516 39	$3,230,174 68	100.00	93.95	3.42	2.63
According to Boroughs.							
$2,155,665 71	$590,509 22	$2,746,174 93	$1,502,444 50	67.63	94.88	3.31	1.81
246,518 89	53,578 19	300,097 08	275,611 55	6.52	92.80	3.76	3.44
718,447 36	335,249 43	1,053,696 79	1,050,883 94	20.37	91.58	4.21	4.21
79,158 54	3,533 28	82,691 82	327,370 40	4.47	92.52	1.51	5.97
18,855 77	....	18,855 77	73,864 29	1.01	92.56	1.52	5.92
$3,218,646 27	$982,870 12	$4,201,516 39	$3,230,174 68	100.00	93.95	3.42	2.63
and General Character of Taxable Property.							
$280,876 47	....	$280,876 47	$184,607 87	58.28	99.35	.39	.26
142,680 30	....	142,680 30	2,852 54	.24	50.70	48.33	.97
1,425,338 02	$590,509 22	2,015,847 24	16,898 52	4.57	63.76	35.93	.31
306,770 92	....	306,770 92	1,298,085 57	4.54	71.21	5.50	23.29
$2,155,665 71	$590,509 22	$2,746,174 93	$1,502,444 50	67.63	94.88	3.31	1.81
$12,555 29	....	$12,555 29	$159,192 48	5.61	97.51	.18	2.31
34,007 14	....	34,007 14	1,689 78	.40	92.71	6.94	.35
127,455 90	$53,578 19	181,034 09	594 79	.32	53.37	46.48	.15
72,500 56	....	72,500 56	114,134 50	.19	20.32	30.95	48.73
$246,518 89	$53,578 19	$300,097 08	$275,611 55	6.52	92.80	3.76	3.44
$43,761 68	....	$43,761 68	$126,709 94	17.55	99.21	.20	.59
50,568 23	....	50,568 23	10,788 36	.23	78.08	18.07	3.85
462,361 71	$335,249 43	797,611 14	65,258 48	1.40	49.84	46.37	3.79
161,755 74	....	161,755 74	848,127 16	1.19	31.09	11.04	57.87
$718,447 36	$335,249 43	$1,053,696 79	$1,050,883 94	20.37	91.58	4.21	4.21
$9,099 81	....	$9,099 81	$186,586 04	3.97	95.98	.19	3.83
2,603 11	....	2,603 11	5,621 43	.15	95.58	1.40	3.02
59,100 07	$3,533 28	62,633 35	20,648 97	.21	67.55	24.40	8.05
8,355 55	....	8,355 55	114,513 96	.14	26.37	5.01	68.62
$79,158 54	$3,533 28	$82,691 82	$327,370 40	4.47	92.52	1.51	5.97
$9,240 10	....	$9,240 10	$36,511 69	.90	95.86	.84	3.30
3,372 91	....	3,372 91	257 39	.03	90.47	8.86	.67
3,420 36	....	3,420 36	22,231 06	.04	45.26	7.30	47.44
2,822 40	....	2,822 40	14,864 15	.04	68.40	5.04	26.56
$18,855 77	....	$18,855 77	$73,864 29	1.01	92.56	1.52	5.92

Part I-A—Tax Levy of 1909, Supporting and Amplifying Totals Shown in Part I Classified According to General Character of Taxable Property and

Class of Tax and Year of Action.	Amount of Levy.	Collections. Total.	Collections. Less Refunds and Over and Double Payments.	Collections. Net.	Discounts.
Real Estate (Lands and Buildings)—					
1909.........	$105,933,728 87	$86,544,457 47	$14,041 81	$86,530,415 66	....
1910.........	....	13,927,432 47	78,894 74	13,848,537 73	....
1911.........	....	2,419,207 74	29,653 08	2,389,554 66	....
1912.........	....	968,550 86	3,463 96	965,086 90	....
1913.........	....	876,967 53	6,727 60	870,239 93	....
1914.........	....	284,987 15	4,234 53	280,752 62	....
Total....	$105,933,728 87	$105,021,603 22	$137,015 72	$104,884,587 50	....
Real Estate of Corporations—					
1909.........	$1,289,192 17	$947,911 37	....	$947,911 37	....
1910.........	....	6,390 43	$151 02	6,239 41	....
1911.........	....	780 08	....	780 08	....
1912.........	....	1,673 84	....	1,673 84	....
1913.........	....	76,837 12	....	76,837 12	....
1914.........	....	1,309 16	....	1,309 16	....
Total....	$1,289,192 17	$1,034,902 00	$151 02	$1,034,750 98	....
Special Franchise—					
1909.........	$8,022,692 92	$1,604,514 91	$1,559 87	$1,602,955 04	....
1910.........	....	2,130,118 39	3,064 14	2,127,054 25	....
1911.........	....	718,055 27	213,028 74	505,026 53	....
1912.........	....	7,778 95	41 95	7,737 00	....
1913.........	....	584,499 05	50 34	584,448 71	....
1914.........	....	9,910 21	616 82	9,293 39	....
Total....	$8,022,692 92	$5,054,876 78	$218,361 86	$4,836,514 92	....
Personal Property—					
1909.........	$7,497,019 70	$4,056,193 17	$960 03	$4,055,233 14	....
1910.........	....	450,837 51	585 10	450,252 41	....
1911.........	....	38,200 50	....	38,200 50	....
1912.........	....	8,486 24	13 90	8,472 34	....
1913.........	....	1,458 84	....	1,458 84	....
1914.........	....	1,471 96	....	1,471 96	....
Total....	$7,497,019 70	$4,556,648 22	$1,559 03	$4,555,089 19	....

Part I-B—Recapitulation—Combining the Four Classes of Tax Shown in the Preceding to year of

Class of Tax and Year of Action.	Amount of Levy.	Total.	Less Refunds and Over and Double Payments.	Net.	Discounts.
Totals for—					
1909.........	$122,742,633 66	$93,153,076 92	$16,561 71	$93,136,515 21	....
1910.........	....	16,514,778 80	82,695 00	16,432,083 80	....
1911.........	....	3,176,243 59	242,681 82	2,933,561 77	....
1912.........	....	986,489 89	3,519 81	982,970 08	....
1913.........	....	1,539,762 54	6,777 94	1,532,984 60	....
1914.........	....	297,678 48	4,851 35	292,827 13	....
Grand Totals..	$122,742,633 66	$115,668,030 22	$357,087 63	$115,310,942 59	....

of Table XI, Showing All Transactions from October 4, 1909, *to December* 31, 1914, *Further Analyzed According to Year in Which Transactions were Made.*

Cancellations.	Deductions Under Section 48, Tax Law.	Total.	Balance Uncollected at December 31, 1914.	Percentages. Net Collections to Levy.	Total Discounts, Cancellations and Deductions to Levy.	Un-Collected Balance to Levy.
$34,002 38	....	$34,002 38	....	....	....	....
45,956 19	....	45,956 19	....	....	....	....
68,370 99	....	68,370 99	....	....	....	....
19,962 73	....	19,962 73	....	....	....	....
55,724 01	....	55,724 01	....	....	....	....
131,517 05	....	131,517 05	....	....	....	....
$355,533 35	....	$355,533 35	$693,608 02	99.01	.33	.66
$159 41	....	$159 41	....	....	....	....
4,881 26	....	4,881 26	....	....	....	....
846 14	....	846 14	....	....	....	....
140,072 97	....	140,072 97	....	....	....	....
15,683 88	....	15,683 88	....	....	....	....
71,588 03	....	71,588 03	....	....	....	....
$233,231 69	....	$233,231 69	$21,209 50	80.27	18.09	1.64
$403,098 76	$329,872 22	$732,970 98	....	....	....	....
493,826 18	298,395 83	792,222 01	....	....	....	....
731,119 13	279,519 65	1,010,638 78	....	....	....	....
347,841 95	29,818 64	377,660 59	....	....	....	....
101,097 24	44,844 27	145,941 51	....	....	....	....
692 80	419 51	1,112 31	....	....	....	....
$2,077,676 06	$982,870 12	$3,060,546 18	$125,631 82	60.29	38.15	1.56
$8,013 83	....	$8,013 83	....	....	....	....
30,383 11	....	30,383 11	....	....	....	....
94,537 16	....	94,537 16	....	....	....	....
219,979 74	....	219,979 74	....	....	....	....
194,761 37	....	194,761 37	....	....	....	....
4,529 96	....	4,529 96	....	....	....	....
$552,205 17	....	$552,205 17	$2,389,725 34	60.76	7.37	31.87

Part (I-A), and Summarizing the Transactions of the Entire Levy of 1909, *According Occurrence.*

Cancellations.	Deductions Under Section 48, Tax Law.	Total.	Balance Uncollected at December 31, 1914.	Net Collections to Levy.	Total Discounts, Cancellations and Deductions to Levy.	Un-Collected Balance to Levy.
$445,274 38	$329,872 22	$775,146 60	....	75.88	.63	....
575,046 74	298,395 83	873,442 57	....	13.39	.71	....
894,873 42	279,519 65	1,174,393 07	....	2.39	.95	....
727,857 39	29,818 64	757,676 03	....	.80	.62	....
367,266 50	44,844 27	412,110 77	....	1.25	.34	....
208,327 84	419 51	208,747 35	....	.24	.17	....
$3,218,646 27	$982,870 12	$4,201,516 39	$3,230,174 68	93.95	3.42	2.63

TABLE XII.—TAX

	Amount of Levy.	Collections. Total.	Collections. Less Refunds and Over and Double Payments.	Collections. Net.	Discounts.
			Part I.—Classified According to General		
Real Estate (Lands and Buildings)	$115,080,167 28	$113,736,201 46	$91,948 65	$113,644,252 81	....
Real Estate of Corporations.	1,555,696 39	1,165,777 67	....	1,165,777 67	....
Special Franchise	8,249,097 11	4,841,471 97	309,628 75	4,531,843 22	....
Personal Property	6,589,809 14	4,622,236 02	1,250 32	4,620,985 70	....
Grand Totals	$131,474,769 92	$124,365,687 12	$402,827 72	$123,962,859 40	....
				Part II.—Classified	
Manhattan	$88,631,999 73	$84,639,507 92	$330,930 91	$84,308,577 01	....
The Bronx	8,814,957 93	8,316,821 34	14,473 79	8,302,347 55	....
Brooklyn	26,558,349 74	24,450,762 32	36,367 43	24,414,394 89	....
Queens	6,154,707 40	5,733,589 33	17,000 48	5,716,588 85	....
Richmond	1,314,755 12	1,225,006 21	4,055 11	1,220,951 10	....
Grand Totals	$131,474,769 92	$124,365,687 12	$402,827 72	$123,962,859 40	....
			Part III.—Classified According to Boroughs		
Manhattan.					
Real Estate (Lands and Buildings)	$77,185,519 60	$76,734,064 16	$50,562 59	$76,683,501 57	....
Real Estate of Corporations.	441,421 36	171,176 71	....	171,176 71	....
Special Franchise	5,766,123 84	3,713,193 50	279,383 16	3,433,810 34	....
Personal Property	5,238,934 93	4,021,073 55	985 16	4,020,088 39	....
Totals	$88,631,999 73	$84,639,507 92	$330,930 91	$84,308,577 01	....
The Bronx.					
Real Estate (Lands and Buildings)	$7,777,682 57	$7,546,395 35	$8,887 18	$7,537,508 17	....
Real Estate of Corporations.	548,718 26	511,324 23	....	511,324 23	....
Special Franchise	352,917 57	215,713 50	5,569 04	210,144 46	....
Personal Property	135,639 53	43,388 26	17 57	43,370 69	....
Totals	$8,814,957 93	$8,316,821 34	$14,473 79	$8,302,347 55	....
Brooklyn.					
Real Estate (Lands and Buildings)	$23,345,975 95	$23,009,275 63	$20,116 78	$22,989,158 85	....
Real Estate of Corporations.	316,604 25	244,146 72	....	244,146 72	....
Special Franchise	1,818,949 58	716,986 81	16,021 81	700,965 00	....
Personal Property	1,076,819 96	480,353 16	228 84	480,124 32	....
Totals	$26,558,349 74	$24,450,762 32	$36,367 43	$24,414,394 89	....
Queens.					
Real Estate (Lands and Buildings)	$5,575,770 51	$5,319,710 17	$11,191 76	$5,308,518 41	....
Real Estate of Corporations.	211,782 38	202,231 74	....	202,231 74	....
Special Franchise	270,129 70	169,679 09	5,808 72	163,870 37	....
Personal Property	97,024 81	41,968 33	....	41,968 33	....
Totals	$6,154,707 40	$5,733,589 33	$17,000 48	$5,716,588 85	....
Richmond.					
Real Estate (Lands and Buildings)	$1,195,218 65	$1,126,756 15	$1,190 34	$1,125,565 81	....
Real Estate of Corporations.	37,170 14	36,898 27	....	36,898 27	....
Special Franchise	40,976 42	25,899 07	2,846 02	23,053 05	....
Personal Property	41,389 91	35,452 72	18 75	35,433 97	....
Totals	$1,314,755 12	$1,225,006 21	$4,055 11	$1,220,951 10	....

LEVY OF 1910.

Cancellations.	Deductions Under Section 48, Tax Law.	Total.	Balance Uncollected at Dec. 31, 1914.	Percentages. Borough and Specific Levy to Total Levy.	Net Collections to Levy.	Total Discounts, Cancellations and Deductions to Levy.	Uncollected Balance to Levy.
Character of	*Taxable Property.*						
$297,306 02	....	$297,306 02	$1,138,608 45	87.53	98.75	.26	.99
311,103 07	....	311,103 07	78,815 65	1.18	74.94	19.99	5.07
997,017 52	$928,992 43	1,926,009 95	1,791,243 94	6.28	54.94	23.35	21.71
510,284 43	....	510,284 43	1,458,539 01	5.01	70.12	7.75	22.13
$2,115,711 04	$928,992 43	$3,044,703 47	$4,467,207 05	100.00	94.29	2.31	3.40
According to Boroughs.							
$1,671,684 80	$514,782 41	$2,186,467 21	$2,136,955 51	67.42	95.12	2.47	2.41
100,546 05	60,834 31	161,380 36	351,230 02	6.70	94.19	1.83	3.98
279,364 28	343,649 32	623,013 60	1,520,941 25	20.20	91.93	2.34	5.73
53,869 35	9,726 39	63,595 74	374,522 81	4.68	92.88	1.03	6.09
10,246 56	....	10,246 56	83,557 46	1.00	92.86	.78	6.36
$2,115,711 04	$928,992 43	$3,044,703 47	$4,467,207 05	100.00	94.29	2.31	3.40
and General Character of Taxable Property.							
$226,486 86	....	$226,486 86	$275,531 17	58.71	99.35	.29	.36
266,053 16	....	266,053 16	4,191 49	.34	38.78	60.28	.94
906,098 91	$514,782 41	1,420,881 32	911,432 18	4.38	59.55	24.64	15.81
273,045 87	....	273,045 87	945,800 67	3.99	76.73	5.22	18.05
$1,671,684 80	$514,782 41	$2,186,467 21	$2,136,955 51	67.42	95.12	2.47	2.41
$10,209 08	....	$10,209 08	$229,965 32	5.91	96.91	.13	2.96
35,623 84	....	35,623 84	1,770 19	.42	93.18	6.50	.32
20,013 75	$60,834 31	80,848 06	61,925 05	.27	59.54	22.91	17.55
34,699 38	....	34,699 38	57,569 46	.10	31.98	25.58	42.44
$100,546 05	$60,834 31	$161,380 36	$351,230 02	6.70	94.19	1.83	3.98
$46,736 29	....	$46,736 29	$310,080 81	17.76	98.47	.20	1.33
6,405 06	....	6,405 06	66,052 47	.24	77.11	2.02	20.87
44,692 82	$343,649 32	388,342 14	729,642 44	1.38	38.54	21.35	40.11
181,530 11	....	181,530 11	415,165 53	.82	44.59	16.86	38.55
$279,364 28	$343,649 32	$623,013 60	$1,520,941 25	20.20	91.93	2.34	5.73
$8,676 77	....	$8,676 77	$258,575 33	4.24	95.21	.15	4.64
2,777 26	....	2,777 26	6,773 38	.16	95.49	1.32	3.19
22,662 49	$9,726 39	32,388 88	73,870 45	.21	60.66	11.99	27.35
19,752 83	....	19,752 83	35,303 65	.07	43.25	20.36	36.39
$53,869 35	$9,726 39	$63,595 74	$374,522 81	4.68	92.88	1.03	6.09
$5,197 02	....	$5,197 02	$64,455 82	.91	94.17	.44	5.39
243 75	....	243 75	28 12	.03	99.27	.66	.07
3,549 55	....	3,549 55	14,373 82	.03	56.26	8.66	35.08
1,256 24	....	1,256 24	4,699 70	.03	85.61	3.04	11.35
$10,246 56	....	$10,246 56	$83,557 46	1.00	92.86	.78	6.36

Part I-A—Tax Levy of 1910—Supporting and Amplifying Totals Shown in Part I Classified According to General Character of Taxable Property, and Further

Class of Tax and Year of Action.	Amount of Levy.	Collections. Total.	Collections. Less Refunds and Over and Double Payments.	Collections. Net.	Discounts.
Real Estate (Lands and Buildings)—					
1910	$115,080,167 28	$92,975,883 44	$1,379 57	$92,974,503 87	....
1911	....	16,120,814 37	77,894 69	16,042,919 68	....
1912	....	2,758,399 22	3,151 97	2,755,247 25	....
1913	....	1,288,317 06	4,540 16	1,283,776 90	....
1914	....	592,787 37	4,982 26	587,805 11	....
Totals	$115,080,167 28	$113,736,201 46	$91,948 65	$113,644,252 81	....
Real Estate of Corporations—					
1910	$1,555,696 39	$1,093,818 26	....	$1,093,818 26	....
1911	....	1,525 38	....	1,525 38	....
1912	....	2,707 18	....	2,707 18	....
1913	....	66,345 13	....	66,345 13	....
1914	....	1,381 72	....	1,381 72	....
Totals	$1,555,696 39	$1,165,777 67	....	$1,165,777 67	....
Special Franchises—					
1910	$8,249,097 11	$3,537,340 36	$21,626 47	$3,515,713 89	....
1911	....	240,066 17	....	240,066 17	....
1912	....	802,646 65	283,861 87	518,784 78	....
1913	....	249,861 94	2,388 00	247,473 94	....
1914	....	11,556 85	1,752 41	9,804 44	....
Totals	$8,249,097 11	$4,841,471 97	$309,628 75	$4,531,843 22	....
Personal Property—					
1910	$6,589,809 14	$4,352,956 33	$612 30	$4,352,344 03	....
1911	....	231,456 69	437 78	231,018 91	....
1912	....	31,081 55	200 24	30,881 31	....
1913	....	5,026 05	....	5,026 05	....
1914	....	1,715 40	....	1,715 40	....
Totals	$6,589,809 14	$4,622,236 02	$1,250 32	$4,620,985 70	....

Part I-B—Recapitulation—Combining the Four Classes of Tax Shown in the Pre According to Year

Class of Tax and Year of Action.	Amount of Levy.	Total.	Less Refunds and Over and Double Payments.	Net.	Discounts.
Totals for—					
1910	$131,474,769 92	$101,959,998 39	$23,618 34	$101,936,380 05	....
1911	....	16,593,862 61	78,332 47	16,515,530 14	....
1912	....	3,594,834 60	287,214 08	3,307,620 52	....
1913	....	1,609,550 18	6,928 16	1,602,622 02	....
1914	....	607,441 34	6,734 67	600,706 67	....
Grand Totals.	$131,474,769 92	$124,365,687 12	$402,827 72	$123,962,859 40	....

of Table XII, Showing All Transactions from October 3, 1910, to December 31, 1914, Analyzed According to Year in Which Transactions Were Made.

Cancellations.	Deductions Under Section 48, Tax Law.	Total.	Balance Uncollected at December 31, 1914.	Percentages. Net Collections to Levy.	Total Discounts, Cancellations and Deductions to Levy.	Un-Collected Balance to Levy.
$55,908 80	....	$55,908 80	....	....	....	....
106,123 94	....	106,123 94	....	....	....	....
38,325 40	....	38,325 40	....	....	....	....
39,862 84	....	39,862 84	....	....	....	....
57,085 04	....	57,085 04	....	....	....	....
$297,306 02	....	$297,306 02	$1,138,608 45	98.75	.26	.99
....	....	....	....	....	....	....
$118,922 23	....	$118,922 23	....	....	....	....
152,663 18	....	152,663 18	....	....	....	....
14,001 89	....	14,001 89	....	....	....	....
25,515 77	....	25,515 77	....	....	....	....
$311,103 07	....	$311,103 07	$78,815 65	74.93	20.00	5.07
....	$391,667 91	$391,667 91	....	....	....	....
$68,851 72	286,359 61	355,211 33	....	....	....	....
716,870 23	158,236 22	875,106 45	....	....	....	....
50,512 79	92,127 50	142,640 29	....	....	....	....
160,782 78	601 19	161,383 97	....	....	....	....
$997,017 52	$928,992 43	$1,926,009 95	$1,791,243 94	54.95	23.34	21.71
$24,112 37	....	$24,112 37	....	....	....	....
36,129 67	....	36,129 67	....	....	....	....
13,046 66	....	13,046 66	....	....	....	....
418,932 32	....	418,932 32	....	....	....	....
18,063 41	....	18,063 41	....	....	....	....
$510,284 43	....	$510,284 43	$1,458,539 01	70.12	7.74	22.14

ceding Part (I-A), and Summarizing the Transactions of the Entire Levy of 1910. of Occurrence.

Cancellations.	Deductions Under Section 48, Tax Law.	Total.	Balance Uncollected at December 31, 1914.	Net Collections to Levy.	Total Discounts, Cancellations and Deductions to Levy.	Un-Collected Balance to Levy.
$80,021 17	$391,667 91	$471,689 08	....	77.50	.36	....
330,027 56	286,359 61	616,387 17	....	12.58	.47	....
920,905 47	158,236 22	1,079,141 69	....	2.52	.82	....
523,309 84	92,127 50	615,437 34	....	1.23	.47	....
261,447 00	601 19	262,048 19	....	.46	.19	....
$2,115,711 04	$928,992 43	$3,044,703 47	$4,467,207 05	94.29	2.31	3.40

TABLE XIII.—TAX

	Amount of Levy.	Collections. Total.	Collections. Less Refunds and Over and Double Payments.	Collections. Net.	Discounts.
			Part I.—Classified According to General		
Real Estate (Lands and Buildings	$124,845,014 59	$122,565,442 66	$124,851 72	$122,440,590 94	....
Real Estate of Corporations	2,881,065 74	2,592,410 74	....	2,592,410 74	....
Special Franchise	8,325,934 55	5,038,821 15	75,786 06	4,963,035 09	....
Personal Property	6,185,744 49	4,392,497 89	3,270 11	4,389,227 78	....
Grand Totals	$142,237,759 37	$134,589,172 44	$203,907 89	$134,385,264 55	....
				Part II.—Classified	
Manhattan	$91,767,837 49	$88,148,330 16	$121,698 55	$88,026,631 61	....
The Bronx	10,510,054 92	9,828,435 95	13,818 99	9,814,616 96	....
Brooklyn	30,624,850 36	28,146,484 15	51,209 09	28,095,275 06	....
Queens	7,846,563 47	7,100,955 06	13,858 36	7,087,096 70	....
Richmond	1,488,453 13	1,364,967 12	3,322 90	1,361,644 22	....
Grand Totals	$142,237,759 37	$134,589,172 44	$203,907 89	$134,385,264 55	....
			Part III.—Classified According to Borough		
Manhattan.					
Real Estate (Lands and Buildings)	$79,794,716 27	$79,248,231 44	$66,779 93	$79,181,451 51	....
Real Estate of Corporations	1,389,490 88	1,230,244 94	....	1,230,244 94	....
Special Franchise	5,592,049 49	3,867,555 98	51,902 65	3,815,653 33	....
Personal Property	4,991,580 85	3,802,297 80	3,015 97	3,799,281 83	....
Total	$91,767,837 49	$88,148,330 16	$121,698 55	$88,026,631 61	....
The Bronx.					
Real Estate (Lands and Buildings)	$9,313,550 44	$8,912,452 72	$8,635 37	$8,903,817 35	....
Real Estate of Corporations	637,902 63	600,787 53	....	600,787 53	....
Special Franchise	472,710 31	271,175 00	5,183 62	265,991 38	....
Personal Property	85,891 54	44,020 70	....	44,020 70	....
Total	$10,510,054 92	$9,828,435 95	$13,818 99	$9,814,616 96	....
Brooklyn.					
Real Estate (Lands and Buildings)	$27,303,589 38	$26,634,230 67	$37,243 29	$26,596,987 38	....
Real Estate of Corporations	411,525 48	339,085 22	....	339,085 22	....
Special Franchise	1,929,473 88	704,005 31	13,763 75	690,241 56	....
Personal Property	980,261 62	469,162 95	202 05	468,960 90	....
Total	$30,624,850 36	$28,146,484 15	$51,209 09	$28,095,275 06	....
Queens.					
Real Estate (Lands and Buildings)	$7,072,959 77	$6,513,225 14	$9,760 34	$6,503,464 80	....
Real Estate of Corporations	396,098 59	376,253 97	....	376,253 97	....
Special Franchise	284,784 42	167,244 76	4,045 93	163,198 83	....
Personal Property	92,720 69	44,231 19	52 09	44,179 10	....
Total	$7,846,563 47	$7,100,955 06	$13,858 36	$7,087,096 70	....
Richmond.					
Real Estate (Lands and Buildings)	$1,360,198 73	$1,257,302 69	$2,432 79	$1,254,869 90	....
Real Estate of Corporations	46,048 16	46,039 08	....	46,039 08	....
Special Franchise	46,916 45	28,840 10	890 11	27,949 99	....
Personal Property	35,289 79	32,785 25	....	32,785 25	....
Total	$1,488,453 13	$1,364,967 12	$3,322 90	$1,361,644 22	....

LEVY OF 1911.

Cancellations.	Deductions Under Section 48, Tax Law.	Total.	Balance Uncollected at Dec. 31, 1914.	Percentages. Borough and Specific Levy to Total Levy.	Net Collections to Levy.	Total Discounts, Cancellations and Deductions to Levy.	Uncollected Balance to Levy.
Character of Taxable Property.							
$303,022 16	....	$303,022 16	$2,101,401 49	87.77	98.08	.24	1.68
193,855 82	....	193,855 82	94,799 18	2.03	89.98	6.73	3.29
664,326 18	$979,360 45	1,643,686 63	1,719,212 83	5.85	59.61	19.74	20.65
508,715 25	....	508,715 25	1,287,801 46	4.35	70.96	8.22	20.82
$1,669,919 41	$979,360 45	$2,649,279 86	$5,203,214 96	100.00	94.48	1.86	3.66
According to Boroughs.							
$1,186,791 70	$562,774 68	$1,749,566 38	$1,991,639 50	64.52	95.92	1.91	2.17
123,119 65	58,292 15	181,411 80	514,026 16	7.39	93.38	1.73	4.89
303,965 55	346,426 93	650,392 48	1,879,182 82	21.53	91.74	2.12	6.14
49,481 25	11,866 69	61,347 94	698,118 83	5.51	90.32	.78	8.90
6,561 26	....	6,561 26	120,247 65	1.05	91.48	.44	8.08
$1,669,919 41	$979,360 45	$2,649,279 86	$5,203,214 96	100.00	94.48	1.86	3.66
and General Character of Taxable Property.							
$155,683 76	....	$155,683 76	$457,581 00	56.10	99.23	.19	.58
154,267 80	....	154,267 80	4,978 14	.98	88.55	11.10	.35
546,765 12	$562,774 68	1,109,539 80	666,856 36	3.93	68.23	19.84	11.93
330,075 02	....	330,075 02	862,224 00	3.51	76.12	6.61	17.27
$1,186,791 70	$562,774 68	$1,749,566 38	$1,991,639 50	64.52	95.92	1.91	2.17
$22,011 49	....	$22,011 49	$387,721 60	6.55	95.60	.24	4.16
35,035 22	....	35,035 22	2,079 88	.45	94.18	5.49	.33
54,390 04	$58,292 15	112,682 19	94,036 74	.33	56.27	23.84	19.89
11,682 90	....	11,682 90	30,187 94	.06	51.25	13.60	35.15
$123,119 65	$58,292 15	$181,411 80	$514,026 16	7.39	93.38	1.73	4.89
$106,610 18	....	$106,610 18	$599,991 82	19.20	97.41	.39	2.20
1,956 82	....	1,956 82	70,483 44	.29	82.39	.48	17.13
43,576 49	$346,426 93	390,003 42	849,228 90	1.36	35.77	20.21	44.02
151,822 06	....	151,822 06	359,478 66	1.68	47.84	15.49	36.67
$303,965 55	$346,426 93	$650,392 48	$1,879,182 82	21.53	91.74	2.12	6.14
$14,262 32	....	$14,262 39	$555,232 65	4.97	91.95	.20	7.85
2,595 98	....	2,595 98	17,248 64	.28	94.99	.66	4.35
17,941 77	$11,866 69	29,808 46	91,777 13	.20	57.31	10.47	32.22
14,681 18	....	14,681 18	33,860 41	.06	47.65	15.83	36.52
$49,481 25	$11,866 69	$61,347 94	$698,118 83	5.51	90.32	.78	8.90
$4,454 41	....	$4,454 41	$100,874 42	.96	92.26	.33	7.41
....	....	....	9 08	.03	99.98	....	.02
1,652 76	....	1,652 76	17,313 70	.04	59.58	3.52	36.90
454 09	....	454 09	2,050 45	.02	92.90	1.29	5.81
$6,561 26	....	$6,561 26	$120,247 65	1.05	91.48	.44	8.08

Part I-A—Tax Levy, 1911, *Supporting and Amplifying Totals Shown in Part I of Classified According to General Character of Taxable Property,*

Class of Tax and Year of Action.	Amount of Levy.	Collections. Total.	Collections. Less Refunds and Over and Double Payments.	Collections. Net.	Discounts.
Real Estate (Lands and Buildings)—					
1911.........	$124,845,014 59	$101,266,484 75	$2,652 62	$101,263,832 13	....
1912.........	....	17,188,229 66	80,068 66	17,108,161 00	....
1913.........	....	2,825,919 45	28,025 36	2,797,894 09	....
1914.........	....	1,284,808 80	14,105 08	1,270,703 72	....
Totals...	$124,845,014 59	$122,565,442 66	$124,851 72	$122,440,590 94	....
Real Estate of Corporations—					
1911.........	$2,881,065 74	$2,517,447 95	....	$2,517,447 95	....
1912.........	....	5,115 02	....	5,115 02	....
1913.........	....	68,661 77	....	68,661 77	....
1914.........	....	1,186 00	....	1,186 00	....
Totals...	$2,881,065 74	$2,592,410 74	....	$2,592,410 74	....
Special Franchise—					
1911.........	$8,325,934 55	$3,803,031 99	$890 11	$3,802,141 88	....
1912.........	....	1,000,928 35	6,050 97	994,877 38	....
1913.........	....	234,812 28	68,844 98	165,967 30	....
1914.........	....	48.53	....	48 53	....
Totals...	$8,325,934 55	$5,038,821 15	$75,786 06	$4,963,035 09	....
Personal Property—					
1911.........	$6,185,744 49	$4,127,735 77	$3,015 97	$4,124,719 80	....
1912.........	....	221,394 40	236 57	221,157 83	....
1913.........	....	34,304 51	....	34,304 51	....
1914.........	....	9,063 21	17 57	9,045 64	....
Totals...	$6,185,744 49	$4,392,497 89	$3,270 11	$4,389,227 78	....

Part I-B—Recapitulation, Combining the Four Classes of Tax Shown in the Pre According to

Class of Tax and Year of Action.	Amount of Levy.	Collections. Total.	Collections. Less Refunds and Over and Double Payments.	Collections. Net.	Discounts.
Totals for—					
1911.........	$142,237,759 37	$111,714,700 46	$6,558 70	$111,708,141 76	....
1912.........	....	18,415,667 43	86,356 20	18,329,311 23	....
1913.........	....	3,163,698 01	96,870 34	3,066,827 67	....
1914.........	....	1,295,106 54	14,122 65	1,280,983 89	....
Grand Totals..	$142,237,759 37	$134,589,172 44	$203,907 89	$134,385,264 55	....

TABLE XIV.—TAX

Part I.—Classified According to General

	Amount of Levy.	Collections. Total.	Collections. Less Refunds and Over and Double Payments.	Collections. Net.	Discounts.
Real Estate (Lands and Buildings)	$133,946,733 95	$130,086,136 22	$142,615 67	$129,943,520 55	$285,499 85
Real Estate of Corporations..	3,109,931 58	2,769,951 40	63 73	2,769,887 67	12,779 61
Special Franchise	7,602,095 47	5,157,121 34	1,127 18	5,155,994 16	19,239 31
Personal Property	6,297,944 75	4,439,126 38	2,719 61	4,436,406 77	....
Grand Totals.......	$150,956,705 75	$142,452,335 34	$146,526 19	$142,305,809 15	$317,518 77

Table XIII, Showing All Transactions from October 2, 1911, to December 31, 1914, and Further Analyzed According to Year in Which Transactions Were Made.

Cancellations.	Deductions Under Section 48, Tax Law.	Total.	Balance Uncollected at December 31, 1914.	Percentages. Net Collections to Levy.	Total Discounts, Cancellations and Deductions to Levy.	Un-Collected Balance to Levy.
$37,528 52	....	$37,528 52	....	....	....	....
90,984 17	....	90,984 17	....	....	....	....
80,655 28	....	80,655 28	....	....	....	....
93,854 19	....	93,854 19	....	....	....	....
$303,022 16	....	$303,022 16	$2,101,401 49	98.08	.24	1.68
....	....	....	....	....	....	....
$5,084 65	....	$5,084 65	....	....	....	....
15,405 98	....	15,405 98	....	....	....	....
173,365 19	....	173,365 19	....	....	....	....
$193,855 82	....	$193,855 82	$94,799 18	89.98	6.73	3.29
$3,140 17	$717,840 24	$720,980 41	....	....	....	....
372,985 69	200,732 05	573,717 74	....	....	....	....
188,018 91	60,190 46	248,209 37	....	....	....	....
100,181 41	597 70	100,779 11	....	....	....	....
$664,326 18	$979,360 45	$1,643,686 63	$1,719,212 83	59.61	19.74	20.65
$14,427 53	....	$14,427 53	....	....	....	....
12,331 67	....	12,331 67	....	....	....	....
315,053 20	....	315,053 20	....	....	....	....
166,902 85	....	166,902 85	....	....	....	....
$508,715 25	....	$508,715 25	$1,287,801 46	70.96	8.22	20.82

ceding Part (I-A) and Summarizing the Transactions of the Entire Levy of 1911, Year of Occurrence.

Cancellations.	Deductions Under Section 48, Tax Law.	Total.	Balance Uncollected at December 31, 1914.	Net Collections to Levy.	Total Discounts, Cancellations and Deductions to Levy.	Un-Collected Balance to Levy.
$55,096 22	$717,840 24	$772,936 46	....	78.54	.54	....
481,386 18	200,732 05	682,118 23	....	12.89	.48	....
599,133 37	60,190 46	659,323 83	....	2.15	.46	....
534,303 64	597 70	534,901 34	....	.90	.38	....
$1,669,919 41	$979,360 45	$2,649,279 86	$5,203,214 96	94.48	1.86	3.66

Levy of 1912.

Cancellations.	Deductions Under Section 48, Tax Law.	Total.	Balance Uncollected at Dec. 31, 1914.	Percentages. Borough and Specific Levy to Total Levy.	Net Collections to Levy.	Total Discounts, Cancellations and Deductions to Levy.	Un-collected Balance to Levy.
Character of	*Taxable Property.*						
$282,289 86	....	$567,789 71	$3,435,423 69	88.73	97.02	.42	2.56
204,345 28	....	217,124 89	122,919 02	2.06	89.07	6.98	3.95
91,744 18	$647,361 39	758,344 88	1,687,756 43	5.04	67.82	9.97	22.21
341,411 69	....	341,411 69	1,520,126 29	4.17	70.44	5.42	24.14
$919,791 01	$647,361 39	$1,884,671 17	$6,766,225 43	100.00	94.27	1.25	4.48

	Amount of Levy.	Collections.			Discounts.
		Total.	Less Refunds and Over and Double Payments.	Net.	
				Part II.—Classified	
Manhattan	$97,300,581 51	$93,491,889 58	$76,763 01	$93,415,126 57	$215,006 37
The Bronx	11,366,058 44	10,493,448 69	11,090 71	10,482,357 98	21,945 43
Brooklyn	32,229,304 15	29,590,619 29	47,849 80	29,542,769 49	60,631 45
Queens	8,521,896 82	7,527,105 00	8,745 87	7,518,359 13	16,716 91
Richmond	1,538,864 83	1,349,272 78	2,076 80	1,347,195 98	3,218 61
Grand Totals.......	$150,956,705 75	$142,452,335 34	$146,526 19	$142,305,809 15	$317,518 77
		Part III.—Classified	*According*	*to*	*Boroughs*
Manhattan.					
Real Estate (Lands and Buildings)	$85,564,598 36	$84,402,589 80	$75,432 53	$84,327,157 27	$192,597 41
Real Estate of Corporations..	1,500,728 77	1,319,564 65	35 68	1,319,528 97	5,198 91
Special Franchise	5,084,409 78	3,891,808 18	....	3,891,808 18	17,210 05
Personal Property	5,150,844 60	3,877,926 95	1,294 80	3,876,632 15	....
Totals	$97,300,581 51	$93,491,889 58	$76,763 01	$93,415,126 57	$215,006 37
The Bronx.					
Real Estate (Lands and Buildings)	$10,168,471 56	$9,544,434 16	$10,999 18	$9,533,434 98	$17,251 75
Real Estate of Corporations..	687,005 59	638,630 48	....	638,630 48	3,335 69
Special Franchise	426,489 54	268,118 64	03	268,118 61	1,357 99
Personal Property	84,091 75	42,265 41	91 50	42,173 91	....
Totals	$11,366,058 44	$10,493,448 69	$11,090 71	$10,482,357 98	$21,945 43
Brooklyn.					
Real Estate (Lands and Buildings)	$29,102,385 47	$28,021,786 13	$46,488 44	$27,975,297 69	$58,453 65
Real Estate of Corporations..	445,900 78	363,157 26	28 05	363,129 21	1,977 59
Special Franchise	1,769,319 01	772,993 31	....	....	200 21
Personal Property	911,698 89	432,682 59	1,333 31	431,349 28	....
Totals	$32,229,304 15	$29,590,619 29	$47,849 80	$29,542,769 49	$60,631 45
Queens.					
Real Estate (Lands and Buildings)	$7,699,263 21	$6,872,776 73	$8,745 87	$6,864,030 86	$14,499 74
Real Estate of Corporations..	428,344 84	403,722 06	....	403,722 06	1,820 86
Special Franchise	276,588 57	195,263 61	....	195,263 61	396 31
Personal Property	117,700 20	55,342 60	....	55,342 60	....
Totals ....;	$8,521,896 82	$7,527,105 00	$8,745 87	$7,518,359 13	$16,716 91
Richmond.					
Real Estate (Lands and Buildings)	$1,412,015 35	$1,244,549 40	$949 65	$1,243,599 75	$2,697 30
Real Estate of Corporations..	47,951 60	44,876 95	....	44,876 95	446 56
Special Franchise	45,288 57	28,937 60	1,127 15	27,810 45	74 75
Personal Property	33,609 31	30,908 83	....	30,908 83	....
Totals	$1,538,864 83	$1,349,272 78	$2,076 80	$1,347,195 98	$3,218 61

Part I-A—Tax Levy of 1912, *Supporting and Amplifying Totals Shown in Part I Classified According to General Character of Taxable Property, and*

Class of Tax and Year of Action.	Amount of Levy.	Collections.			Discounts.
		Total.	Less Refunds and Over and Double Payments.	Net.	
Real Estate (Lands and Buildings)—					
1912.........	$133,946,733 95	$113,760,315 56	$8,653 90	$113,751,661 66	$285,499 85
1913.........	....	13,756,767 52	115,984 58	13,640,782 94	....
1914.........	....	2,569,053 14	17,977 19	2,551,075 95	....
Totals...	$133,946,733 95	$130,086,136 22	$142,615 67	$129,943,520 55	$285,499 85

Cancellations.	Deductions Under Section 48, Tax Law.	Total.	Balance Uncollected at Dec. 31, 1914.	Percentages. Borough and Specific Levy to Total Levy.	Net Collections to Levy.	Total Discounts, Cancellations and Deductions to Levy.	Uncollected Balance to Levy.
According to Boroughs.							
$580,482 68	$394,510 06	$1,189,999 11	$2,695,455 83	64.46	96.00	1.23	2.77
57,453 64	44,455 81	123,854 88	759,845 58	7.53	92.22	1.09	6.69
232,386 35	194,750 95	487,768 75	2,198,765 91	21.35	91.66	1.51	6.83
43,513 34	13,644 57	73,874 82	929,662 87	5.64	88.22	.87	10.91
5,955 00	....	9,173 61	182,495 24	1.02	87.51	.59	11.90
$919,791 01	$647,361 39	$1,884,671 17	$6,766,225 43	100.00	94.27	1.25	4.48
and General Character of Taxable Property.							
$121,308 42	....	$313,905 83	$923,535 26	56.68	98.55	.37	1.08
160,855 39	....	166,054 30	15,145 50	1.00	87.92	11.07	1.01
88,481 42	$394,510 06	500,201 53	692,400 07	3.37	76.54	9.84	13.62
209,837 45	....	209,837 45	1,064,375 00	3.41	75.26	4.08	20.66
$580,482 68	$394,510 06	$1,189,999 11	$2,695,455 83	64.46	96.00	1.23	2.77
$15,060 78	....	$32,312 53	$602,724 05	6.74	93.76	.31	5.93
37,240 50	....	40,576 19	7,798 92	.45	92.96	5.91	1.13
1,665 30	$44,455 81	47,479 10	110,891 83	.28	62.86	11.13	26.01
3,487 06	....	3,487 06	38,430 78	.06	50.15	4.15	45.70
$57,453 64	$44,455 81	$123,854 88	$759,845 58	7.53	92.22	1.09	6.69
$109,695 34	....	$168,148 99	$958,938 79	19.28	96.13	.58	3.29
3,398 72	....	5,376 31	77,395 26	.30	81.44	1.20	17.36
470 31	$194,750 95	195,421 47	800,904 23	1.17	43.69	11.04	45.27
118,821 98	....	118,821 98	361,527 63	.60	47.31	13.03	39.66
$232,386 35	$194,750 95	$487,768 75	$2,198,765 91	21.35	91.66	1.51	6.83
$31,446 62	....	$45,946 36	$789,285 99	5.10	89.15	.60	10.25
2,820 72	....	4,641 58	19,981 20	.28	94.26	1.08	4.66
....	$13,644 57	14,040 88	67,284 08	.18	70.60	5.07	24.33
9,246 00	....	9,246 00	53,111 60	.08	47.02	7.86	45.12
$43,513 34	$13,644 57	$73,874 82	$929,662 87	5.64	88.22	.87	10.91
$4,778 70	....	$7,476 00	$160,939 60	.94	88.07	.53	11.40
29 95	....	476 51	2,598 14	.03	93.59	.99	5.42
1,127 15	....	1,201 90	16,276 22	.03	61.41	2.65	35.94
19 20	....	19 20	2,681 28	.02	91.97	.06	7.97
$5,955 00	....	$9,173 61	$182,495 24	1.02	87.51	.59	11.90

of Table XIV, Showing All Transactions from May 1, 1912, *to December* 31, 1914, *Further Analyzed According to Year in Which Transactions Were Made.*

Cancellations.	Deductions Under Section 48, Tax Law.	Total.	Balance Uncollected at December 31, 1914.	Percentages. Net Collections to Levy.	Total Discounts, Cancellations and Deductions to Levy.	Un-Collected Balance to Levy.
$111,266 21	....	$396,766 06	....	....	....	....
113,510 54	....	113,510 54	....	....	....	....
57,513 11	....	57,513 11	....	....	....	....
$282,289 86	....	$567,789 71	$3,435,423 69	97.01	.42	2.57

Class of Tax and Year of Action.	Amount of Levy.	Collections.			Discounts.
		Total.	Less Refunds and Over and Double Payments.	Net.	
Real Estate of Corporations—					
1912.........	$3,109,931 58	$2,585,631 51	....	$2,585,631 51	$12,779 61
1913.........	....	182,675 22	$35 68	182,639 54	....
1914.........	....	1,644 67	28 05	1,616 62	....
Totals...	$3,109,931 58	$2,769,951 40	$63 73	$2,769,887 67	$12,779 61
Special Franchise—					
1912.........	$7,602,095 47	$4,921,986 05	$1,127 15	$4,920,858 90	$19,239 31
1913.........	....	232,637 34	03	232,637 31	....
1914.........	....	2,497 95	....	2,497 95	....
Totals...	$7,602,095 47	$5,157,121 34	$1,127 18	$5,155,994 16	$19,239 31
Personal Property—					
1912.........	$6,297,944 75	$4,239,230 05	$1,760 30	$4,237,469 75	....
1913.........	....	159,646 04	755 48	158,890 56	....
1914.........	....	40,250 29	203 83	40,046 46	....
Totals...	$6,297,944 75	$4,439,126 38	$2,719 61	$4,436,406 77	....

Part I-B—Recapitulation—Combining the Four Classes of Tax Shown in the Preced According to Year

Class of Tax and Year of Action.	Amount of Levy.	Total.	Less Refunds and Over and Double Payments.	Net.	Discounts.
Totals for—					
1912.........	$150,956,705 75	$125,507,163 17	$11,541 35	$125,495,621 82	$317,518 77
1913.........	....	14,331,726 12	116,775 77	14,214,950 35	....
1914.........	....	2,613,446 05	18,209 07	2,595,236 98	....
Grand Totals.	$150,956,705 75	$142,452,335 34	$146,526 19	$142,305,809 15	$317,518 77

TABLE XV.—TAX

	Amount of Levy.	Collections.			Discounts.
		Total.	Less Refunds and Over and Double Payments.	Net.	
			Part I.—Classified According to General		
Real Estate (Lands and Buildings)	$134,590,929 55	$127,894,602 84	$112,784 55	$127,781,818 29	$258,380 34
Real Estate of Corporations.	3,290,268 45	2,957,836 06	18 56	2,957,817 50	5,955 66
Special Franchise	7,991,775 16	4,817,602 84	2,159 50	4,815,443 34	14,594 07
Personal Property	5,913,295 25	3,960,477 24	2,083 40	3,958,393 84	......
Grand Totals	$151,786,268 41	$139,630,518 98	$117,046 01	$139,513,472 97	$278,930 07
					Part II.—Classified
Manhattan	$97,603,783 92	$91,364,314 66	$70,160 64	$91,294,154 02	$191,790 83
The Bronx	11,681,997 76	10,459,766 35	6,267 75	10,453,498 60	17,426 69
Brooklyn	31,936,685 12	28,966,171 23	34,929 05	28,931,242 18	51,243 45
Queens	8,963,767 19	7,531,047 80	4,940 44	7,526,107 36	15,241 74
Richmond	1,600,034 42	1,309,218 94	748 13	1,308,470 81	3,227 36
Grand Totals	$151,786,268 41	$139,630,518 98	$117,046 01	$139,513,472 97	$278,930 07

Cancellations.	Deductions Under Section 48, Tax Law.	Total.	Balance Uncollected at December 31, 1914.	Percentages. Net Collections to Levy.	Total Discounts, Cancellations and Deductions to Levy.	Un-Collected Balance to Levy.
$2,127 34	....	$14,906 95	....	....	....	....
16,456 86	....	16,456 86	....	....	....	....
185,761 08	....	185,761 08	....	....	....	....
$204,345 28	....	$217,124 89	$122,919 02	89.07	6.98	3.95
$35,868 00	$602,286 45	$657,393 76	....	....	....	....
4,251 88	44,659 53	48,911 41	....	....	....	....
51,624 30	415 41	52,039 71	....	....	....	....
$91,744 18	$647,361 39	$758,344 88	$1,687,756 43	67.82	9.98	22.20
$54,762 80	....	$54,762 80	....	....	....	....
5,407 36	....	5,407 36	....	....	....	....
281,241 53	....	281,241 53	....	....	....	....
$341,411 69	....	$341,411 69	$1,520,126 29	70.44	5.42	24.14

ing Part (I-A), and Summarizing the Transactions of the Entire Levy of 1912, *of Occurrence.*

$204,024 35	$602,286 45	$1,123,829 57	....	83.14	.75	....
139,626 64	44,659 53	184,286 17	....	9.41	.12	....
576,140 02	415 41	576,555 43	....	1.72	.38	....
$919,791 01	$647,361 39	$1,884,671 17	$6,766,225 43	94.27	1.25	4.48

Levy of 1913.

Cancellations.	Deductions Under Section 48, Tax Law.	Total.	Balance Uncollected at Dec. 31, 1914.	Percentages. Borough and Specific Levy to Total Levy.	Net Collections to Levy.	Total Discounts, Cancellations and Deductions to Levy.	Un-collected Balance to Levy.
Character of Taxable Property.							
$216,938 83	....	$475,319 17	$6,333,792 09	88.67	94.94	.35	4.71
37,668 00	....	43,623 66	288,827 29	2.17	89.89	1.33	8.78
....	$967,928 91	982,522 98	2,193,808 84	5.27	60.26	12.29	27.45
51,689 70	....	51,689 70	1,903,211 71	3.89	66.94	.87	32.19
306,296 53	$967,928 91	$1,553,155 51	$10,719,639 93	100.00	91.92	1.02	7.06
According to Boroughs.							
$177,860 11	$545,574 89	$915,225 83	$5,394,404 07	64.30	93.54	.94	5.52
20,606 65	50,173 30	88,206 64	1,140,292 52	7.69	89.48	.76	9.76
64,840 08	355,925 56	472,009 09	2,533,433 85	21.04	90.59	1.48	7.93
33,566 09	16,255 16	65.062 99	1,372,596 84	5.91	83.96	.73	15.31
9,423 60	....	12,650 96	278,912 65	1.06	81.78	.79	17.43
306,296 53	$967,928 91	$1,553,155 51	$10,719,639 93	100.00	91.92	1.02	7.06

	Amount of Levy.	Collections. Total.	Collections. Less Refunds and Over and Double Payments.	Collections. Net.	Discounts.
			Part III.—Classified	*According to*	*Boroughs*
Manhattan.					
Real Estate (Lands and Buildings)	$85,843,779 85	$83,321,191 81	$66,987 54	$83,254,204 27	$175,397 72
Real Estate of Corporations.	1,566,314 93	1,378,033 31	......	1,378,033 31	3,673 41
Special Franchise	5,387,916 03	3,277,978 28	2,159 50	3,225,818 78	12,719 70
Personal Property	4,805,773 11	3,437,111 26	1,013 60	3,436,097 66	......
Totals	$97,603,783 92	$91,364,314 66	$70,160 64	$91,294,154 02	$191,790 83
The Bronx.					
Real Estate (Lands and Buildings)	$10,367,458 75	$9,438,447 38	$6,249 65	$9,432,197 73	$15,818 82
Real Estate of Corporations.	774,513 51	723,275 30	18 10	723,257 20	397 62
Special Franchise	447,823 34	257,079 65	......	257,079 65	1,210 25
Personal Property	92,202 16	40,964 02	......	40,964 02	......
Totals	$11,681,997 76	$10,459,766 35	$6,267 75	$10,453,498 60	$17,426 69
Brooklyn.					
Real Estate (Lands and Buildings)	$28,843,191 25	$27,074,884 69	$33,858 79	$27,041,025 90	$50,736 53
Real Estate of Corporations.	415,846 68	393,230 97	46	393,230 51	231 98
Special Franchise	1,821,155 64	1,092,840 48	......	1,092,840 48	274 94
Personal Property	856,491 55	405,215 09	1,069 80	404,145 29	......
Totals	$31,936,685 12	$28,966,171 23	$34,929 05	$28,931,242 18	$51,243 45
Queens.					
Real Estate (Lands and Buildings)	$8,070,525 29	$6,854,686 62	$4,940 44	$6,849,746 18	$13,743 88
Real Estate of Corporations.	483,108 66	416,187 08	......	416,187 08	1,177 54
Special Franchise	285,427 53	211,296 19	......	211,296 19	320 32
Personal Property	124,705 71	48,877 91	......	48,877 91	......
Totals	$8,963,767 19	$7,531,047 80	$4,940 44	$7,526,107 36	$15,241 74
Richmond.					
Real Estate (Lands and Buildings)	$1,465,974 41	$1,205,392 34	$748 13	$1,204,644 21	$2,683 39
Real Estate of Corporations.	50,484 67	47,109 40	......	47,109 40	475 11
Special Franchise	49,452 62	28,408 24	......	28,408 24	68 86
Personal Property	34,122 72	28,308 96	......	28,308 96	......
Totals	$1,600,034 42	$1,309,218 94	$748 13	$1,308,470 81	$3,227 36

Part I-A—Tax Levy of 1913—*Supporting and Amplifying Totals Shown in Part I of Classified According to General Character of Taxable Property, and*

Class of Tax and Year of Action.	Amount of Levy.	Collections. Total.	Collections. Less Refunds and Over and Double Payments.	Collections. Net.	Discounts.
Real Estate (Lands and Buildings)—					
1913.........	$134,590,929 55	$114,670,374 13	$47,563 83	$114,622,810 30	$258,375 89
1914.........	....	13,224,228 71	65,220 72	13,159,007 99	4 45
Totals...	$134,590,929 55	$127,894,602 84	$112,784 55	$127,781,818 29	$258,380 34
Real Estate of Corporations—					
1913.........	$3,290,268 45	$2,943,004 62	$18 10	$2,942,986 52	$5,955 66
1914.........	....	14,831 44	46	14,830 98	....
Totals...	$3,290,268 45	$2,957,836 06	$18 56	$2,957,817 50	$5,955 66

Cancellations.	Deductions Under Section 48, Tax Law.	Total.	Balance Uncollected at Dec. 31, 1914.	Percentages. Borough and Specific Levy to Total Levy.	Net Collections to Levy.	Total Discounts, Cancellations and Deductions to Levy.	Uncollected Balance to Levy.
and General Character of Taxable Property.							
$129,317 68	....	$304,715 40	$2,284,860 18	56.55	96.98	.36	2.66
5,427 28	....	9,100 69	179,180 93	1.03	87.98	.58	11.44
....	$545,574 89	558,294 59	1,603,802 66	3.55	59.87	10.36	29.77
43,115 15	....	43,115 15	1,326,560 30	3.17	71.50	.90	27.60
$177,860 11	$545,574 89	$915,225 83	$5,394,404 07	64.30	93.54	.94	5.52
$16,657 69	....	$32,476 51	$902,784 51	6.83	90.98	.32	8.70
3,659 36	....	4,056 98	47,199 33	.51	93.38	.53	6.09
....	$50,173 30	51,383 55	139,360 14	.29	57.40	11.48	31.12
289 60	....	289 60	50,948 54	.06	44.43	.31	55.26
$20,606 65	$50,173 30	$88,206 64	$1,140,292 52	7.69	89.48	.76	9.76
$57,488 53	....	$108,225 06	$1,693,940 29	19.00	93.75	.38	5.87
....	....	231 98	22,384 19	.27	94.56	.06	5.38
....	....	356,200 50	372,114 66	1.20	60.01	19.56	20.43
7,351 55	....	7,351 55	444,994 71	.57	47.18	.86	51.96
$64,840 08	....	$472,009 09	$2,533,433 85	21.04	90.59	1.48	7.93
$4,396 93	....	$18,140 81	$1,202,638 30	5.32	84.87	.23	14.90
28,466 16	....	29,643 70	37,277 88	.32	86.16	6.13	7.71
....	$16,255 16	16,575 48	57,555 86	.19	74.03	5.81	20.16
703 00	....	703 00	75,124 80	.08	39.19	.57	60.24
$33,566 09	$16,255 16	$65,062 99	$1,372,596 84	5.91	83.96	.73	15.31
9,078 00	....	$11,761 39	$249,568 81	.97	82.17	.80	17.03
115 20	....	590 31	2,784 96	.04	93.31	1.17	5.52
....	....	68 86	20,975 52	.03	57.44	.14	42.42
230 40	....	230 40	5,583 36	.02	82.97	.67	16.36
$9,423 60	....	$12,650 96	$278,912 65	1.06	81.78	.79	17.43

Table XV, Showing All Transactions from May 1, 1913, to December 31, 1914, Further Analyzed According to Year in Which Transactions were Made.

Cancellations.	Deductions Under Section 48, Tax Law.	Total.	Balance Uncollected at December 31, 1914.	Percentages. Net Collections to Levy.	Total Discounts, Cancellations and Deductions to Levy.	Un-Collected Balance to Levy.
$88,534 80	....	$346,910 69	....	....	....	....
128,404 03	....	128,408 48	....	....	....	....
$216,938 83	....	$475,319 17	$6,333,792 09	94.94	.35	4.71
$31,708 28	....	$37,663 94	....	....	....	....
5,959,72	....	5,959 72	....	....	....	....
$37,668 00	....	$43,623 66	$288,827 29	89.89	1.33	8.78

Class of Tax and Year of Action.	Amount of Levy.	Collections. Total.	Collections. Less Refunds and Over and Double Payments.	Collections. Net.	Discounts.
Special Franchise—					
1913.........	$7,991,775 16	$4,808,074 73	....	$4,808,074 73	$14,594 07
1914.........	....	9,528 11	$2,159 50	7,368 61	....
Totals...	$7,991,775 16	$4,817,602 84	$2,159 50	$4,815,443 34	$14,594 07
Personal Property—					
1913.........	$5,913,295 25	$3,788,298 33	$1,268 90	$3,787,029 43	....
1914.........	....	172,178 91	814 50	171,364 41	....
Totals...	$5,913,295 25	$3,960,477 24	$2,083 40	$3,958,393 84	....

Part I-B—Recapitulation—Combining the Four Classes of Tax Shown in the Preceding to Year of

Totals for—					
1913.........	$151,786,268 41	$126,209,751 81	$48,850 83	$126,160,900 98	$278,925 62
1914.........	....	13,420,767 17	68,195 18	13,352,571 99	4 45
Grand Totals.	$151,786,268 41	$139,630,518 98	$117,046 01	$139,513,472 97	$278,930 07

Table XVI.—Tax

	Amount of Levy.	Collections. Total.	Collections. Less Refunds and Over and Double Payments.	Collections. Net.	Discounts.
			Part I.—Classified According to General		
Real Estate (Lands and Buildings)	$133,831,562 06	$113,400,821 09	$43,894 32	$113,356,926 77	$264,893 87
Real Estate of Corporations..	3,339,684 26	3,043,596 03	....	3,043,596 03	9,493 65
Special Franchise	7,248,956 94	4,138,921 85	....	4,138,921 85	17,714 38
Personal Property	6,083,311 27	3,828,245 75	776 72	3,827,469 03	....
Grand Totals.......	$150,503,514 53	$124,411,584 72	$44,671 04	$124,366,913 68	$292,101 90
				Part II.—Classified	
Manhattan	$96,778,936 70	$83,010,520 80	$40,445 65	$82,970,075 15	$197,340 94
The Bronx	11,759,491 12	9,144,022 64	2,076 17	9,141,946 47	17,195 65
Brooklyn	31,472,676 10	24,783,391 04	2,072 60	24,781,318 44	57,655 85
Queens	8,902,777 94	6,369,191 23	33 30	6,369,157 93	16,468 81
Richmond	1,589,632 67	1,104,459 01	43 32	1,104,415 69	3,440 65
Grand Totals.......	$150,503,514 53	$124,411,584 72	$44,671 04	$124,366,913 68	$292,101 90
			Part III.—Classified According to Boroughs		
Manhattan.					
Real Estate (Lands and Buildings)	$84,982,143 70	$75,329,940 64	$39,931 23	$75,290,009 41	$178,082 01
Real Estate of Corporations..	1,651,463 14	1,465,171 61	....	1,465,171 61	5,117 93
Special Franchise	5,023,054 66	2,867,723 68	....	2,867,723 68	14,141 00
Personal Property	5,122,275 20	3,347,684 87	514 42	3,347,170 45	....
Totals	$96,778,936 70	$83,010,520 80	$40,445 65	$82,970,075 15	$197,340 94

Cancellations.	Deductions Under Section 48, Tax Law.	Total.	Balance Uncollected at December 31, 1914.	Percentages. Net Collections to Levy.	Percentages. Total Discounts, Cancellations and Deductions to Levy.	Percentages. Un-Collected Balance to Levy.
....	$967,517 14	$982,111 21	....	....	....	....
....	411 77	411 77	....	....	....	....
....	$967,928 91	$982,522 98	$2,193,808 84	60.26	12.29	27.45
$38,358 26	....	$38,358 26	....	....	....	....
13,331 44	....	13,331 44	....	....	....	....
$51,689 70	....	$51,689 70	$1,903,211 71	66.94	.87	32.19

Part (I-A), and Summarizing the Transactions of the Entire Levy of 1913, *According Occurrence.*

Cancellations.	Deductions Under Section 48, Tax Law.	Total.	Balance Uncollected at December 31, 1914.	Net Collections to Levy.	Total Discounts, Cancellations and Deductions to Levy.	Un-Collected Balance to Levy.
$158,601 34	$967,517 14	$1,405,044 10	....	83.12	.93	....
147,695 19	411 77	148,111 41	....	8.80	.09	....
$306,296 53	$967,928 91	$1,553,155 51	$10,719,639 93	91.92	1.02	7.06

Levy of 1914.

Cancellations.	Deductions Under Section 48, Tax Law.	Total.	Balance Uncollected at Dec. 31, 1914.	Percentages. Borough and Specific Levy to Total Levy.	Percentages. Net Collections to Levy.	Percentages. Total Discounts, Cancellations and Deductions to Levy.	Percentages. Un-collected Balance to Levy.
Character of Taxable Property.							
$110,411 03	....	$375,304 90	$20,099,330 39	81.34	84.70	.28	15:02
2,947 38	....	12,441 03	283,647 20	1.15	91.14	.37	8.49
....	$968,765 45	986,479 83	2,123,555 26	8.60	57.10	13.61	29.29
53,268 06	....	53,268 06	2,202,574 18	8.91	62.91	.88	36.21
$166,626 47	$968,765 45	$1,427,493 82	$24,709,107 03	100.00	82.64	.95	16.41
According to Boroughs.							
$125,551 41	$541,533 26	$864,425 61	$12,944,435 94	64.30	85.73	.89	13.38
17,468 52	85,515 49	120,179 66	2,497,364 99	7.81	77.74	1.02	21.24
16,021 80	324,948 25	398,625 90	6,292,731 76	20.91	78.74	1.27	19.99
1,880 54	16,768 45	35,117 80	2,498,502 21	5.91	71.54	.40	28.06
5,704 20	....	9,144 85	476,072 13	1.07	69.47	.58	29.95
$166,626 47	$968,765 45	$1,427,493 82	$24,709,107 03	100.00	82.64	.95	16.41

and General Character of Taxable Property.

Cancellations.	Deductions Under Section 48, Tax Law.	Total.	Balance Uncollected at Dec. 31, 1914.	Borough and Specific Levy to Total Levy.	Net Collections to Levy.	Total Discounts, Cancellations and Deductions to Levy.	Un-collected Balance to Levy.
$81,359 35	....	$259,441 36	$9,432,692 93	56.47	88.60	.30	11.10
277 68	....	5,395 61	180,895 92	1.09	88.72	.33	10.95
....	$541,533 26	555,674 26	1,599,656 72	3.34	57.09	11.06	31.85
43,914 38	....	43,914 38	1,731,190 37	3.40	65.34	.86	33.80
$125,551 41	$541,533 26	$864,425 61	$12,944,435 94	64.30	85.73	.89	13.38

	Amount of Levy.	Collections. Total.	Less Refunds and Over and Double Payments.	Net.	Discounts.
The Bronx.					
Real Estate (Lands and Buildings)	$10,432,057 88	$8,177,381 98	$2,008 91	$8,175,373 07	$15,564 91
Real Estate of Corporations..	762,644 90	710,184 41	....	710,184 41	418 27
Special Franchise	462,815 10	215,921 48	....	215,921 48	1,212 47
Personal Property	101,973 24	40,534 77	67 26	40,467 51	....
Totals	$11,759,491 12	$9,144,022 64	$2,076 17	$9,141,946 47	$17,195 65
Brooklyn.					
Real Estate (Lands and Buildings)	$28,915,351 39	$23,190,806 87	$1,877 56	$23,188,929 31	$54,272 35
Real Estate of Corporations..	394,263 30	382,706 44	....	382,706 44	1,778 02
Special Franchise	1,440,013 90	836,429 44	....	836,429 44	1,605 48
Personal Property	723,047 51	373,448 29	195 04	373,253 25	....
Totals	$31,472,676 10	$24,783,391 04	$2,072 60	$24,781,318 44	$57,655 85
Queens.					
Real Estate (Lands and Buildings)	$8,040,300 44	$5,691,442 07	$33 30	$5,691,408 77	$14,099 95
Real Estate of Corporations..	477,976 32	434,991 38	....	434,991 38	1,681 16
Special Franchise	278,028 48	199,382 28	....	199,382 28	687 70
Personal Property	106,472 70	43,375 50	....	43,375 50	....
Totals	$8,902,777 94	$6,369,191 23	$33 30	$6,369,157 93	$16,468 81
Richmond.					
Real Estate (Lands and Buildings)	$1,461,708 65	$1,011,249 53	$43 32	$1,011,206 21	$2,874 65
Real Estate of Corporations..	53,336 60	50,542 19	....	50,542 19	498 27
Special Franchise	45,044 80	19,464 97	....	19,464 97	67 73
Personal Property	29,542 62	23,202 32	....	23,202 32	....
Totals	$1,589,632 67	$1,104,459 01	$43 32	$1,104,415 69	$3,440 65

Part I-A—Tax Levy of 1914. *Supporting and Amplifying Totals Shown in Part I. Classified According to General Character of Taxable Property, and Further*

Class of Tax and Year of Action.	Amount of Levy.	Collections. Total.	Less Refunds and Over and Double Payments.	Net.	Discounts.
Real Estate (Lands and Buildings)— 1914.........	$133,831,562 06	$113,400,821 09	$43,894 32	$113,356,926 77	$264,893 87
Real Estate of Corporations— 1914.........	3,339,684 26	3,043,596 03	....	3,043,596 03	9,493 65
Special Franchise— 1914.........	7,248,956 94	4,138,921 85	....	4,138,921 85	17,714 38
Personal Property— 1914.........	6,083,311 27	3,828,245 75	776 72	3,827,469 03	....
Grand Totals..	$150,503,514 53	$124,411,584 72	$44,671 04	$124,366,913 68	$292,101 90

Cancellations.	Deductions Under Section 48, Tax Law.	Total.	Balance Uncollected at Dec. 31, 1914.	Percentages. Borough and Specific Levy to Total Levy.	Net Collections to Levy.	Total Discounts, Cancellations and Deductions to Levy.	Uncollected Balance to Levy.
$13,654 18	....	$29,219 09	$2,227,465 72	6.93	78.38	.28	21.34
2,469 14	....	2,887 41	49,573 08	.51	93.12	.38	6.50
....	$85,515 49	86,727 96	160,165 66	.31	46.65	18.74	34.61
1,345 20	....	1,345 20	60,160 53	.06	39.68	1.32	59.00
$17,468 52	$85,515 49	$120,179 66	$2,497,364 99	7.81	77.74	1.02	21.24
$8,190 76	....	$62,463 11	$5,663,958 97	19.21	80.20	.22	19.58
200 56	....	1,978 58	9,578 28	.26	97.07	.50	2.43
....	$324,948 25	326,553 73	277,030 73	.96	58.08	22.68	19.24
7,630 48	....	7,630 48	342,163 78	.48	51.62	1.06	47.32
$16,021 80	$324,948 25	$398,625 90	$6,292,731 76	20.91	78.74	1.27	19.99
$1,502 54	....	$15,602 49	$2,333,289 18	5.34	70.78	.20	29.02
....	....	1,681 16	41,303 78	.32	91.01	.35	8.64
....	$16,768 45	17,456 15	61,190 05	.18	71.71	6.28	22.01
378 00	....	378 00	62,719 20	.07	40.74	.35	58.91
$1,880 54	$16,768 45	$35,117 80	$2,498,502 21	5.91	71.54	.40	28.06
$5,704 20	....	$8,578 85	$441,923 59	.98	69.17	.59	30.24
....	....	498 27	2,296 14	.04	94.76	.94	4.30
....	....	67 73	25,512 10	.03	43.21	.15	56.64
....	....	....	6,340 30	.02	78.53	......	21.47
$5,704 20	....	$9,144 85	$476,072 13	1.07	69.47	.58	29.95

of Table XVI., Showing All Transactions from May 1, 1914, *to December* 31, 1914, *Analyzed According to Year in Which Transactions Were Made.*

Cancellations.	Deductions Under Section 48, Tax Law.	Total.	Balance Uncollected at December 31, 1914.	Percentages. Net Collections to Levy.	Total Discounts, Cancellations and Deductions to Levy.	Un-Collected Balance to Levy.
$110,411 03	....	$375,304 90	$20,099,330 39	84.70	.28	15.02
2,947 38	....	12,441 03	283,647 20	91.13	.37	8.50
....	$968,765 45	986,479 83	2,123,555 26	57.10	13.61	29.29
53,268 06	....	53,268 06	2,202,574 18	62.92	.87	36.21
$166,626 47	$968,765 45	$1,427,493 82	$24,709,107 03	82.64	.95	16.41

www.ingramcontent.com/pod-product-compliance
Lightning Source LLC
LaVergne TN
LVHW011119110826
845150LV00008B/2185

* 9 7 8 1 4 2 5 5 0 6 9 3 3 *